ALLEN BARGFREDE

C000225729

MUSIC
LAW IN THE
DIGITAL
AGE

COPYRIGHT ESSENTIALS
FOR TODAY'S MUSIC BUSINESS

To access sample contracts visit:
www.halleonard.com/mylibrary

Enter Code
2713-9625-6254-1869

3RD EDITION

Berklee Press

Editor in Chief: Jonathan Feist
Senior Vice President of Online Learning and Continuing Education/CEO of Berklee Online: Debbie Cavalier
Vice President of Enrollment Marketing and Management: Mike King
Vice President of Academic Strategy: Carin Nuernberg
Editorial Assistant: Brittany McCorriston
Assistants for the First Edition: Mina Cho, Yousun Choi, Martin Fowler, Emily Goldstein, Claudia Obser
Assistants for the Second Edition: Emily Jones, Eloise Kelsey
Cover Designer: Kathy Kikkert

ISBN: 978-1-70515-648-3

Study music online at
online.berklee.edu

HAL•LEONARD®
7777 W. BLUEMOUND RD. P.O. BOX 13819
MILWAUKEE, WISCONSIN 53213

1140 Boylston Street
Boston, MA 02215-3693 USA
(617) 747-2146

Visit Berklee Press Online at
www.berkleepress.com

Visit Hal Leonard Online
www.halleonard.com

Berklee Press, a publishing activity of Berklee College of Music, is a not-for-profit educational publisher.
Available proceeds from the sales of our products are contributed to the scholarship funds of the college.

"If music be the food of love, play on, give me excess of it."

—*William Shakespeare*

CONTENTS

AUTHOR NOTE

This book is designed to serve as a reference guide. It is not intended or designed to serve as a substitute for legal advice. Due to rapid changes in industry law, customs, technology, and legislation, some parts of this book may be outdated even upon publication. The author and publisher make no warranties as to the information contained in this text, and assume no liability if a reader acts upon the information contained herein. If legal advice is required, please consult the services of an attorney or other qualified professional.

ACKNOWLEDGMENTS

I would like to thank Cecily Mak for working diligently with me on the first edition of this book, and Adam Parness for his overwhelming help in proofreading and editing. The development of this book has been a combination of fun, hard work, and a continued learning process that continues with each new edition.

I would also like to acknowledge the following people for their continued inspiration and help on this project: My parents, and my family; all of my friends and colleagues, but especially Derek Crownover, for pushing me to continue and the oft-needed advice, Ken Umezaki and our team at Verifi Media; Roger Brown, Panos Panay, my students, and everyone else at Berklee College of Music in both Boston and Valencia for their support of my career; Chris Bavitz of Harvard Law School, and all of the others with whom I have worked on the Rethink Music initiative since launching it in 2010.

INTRODUCTION

The idea for this book emerged a few years ago when I realized, with my good friend (and co-author on the first edition) Cecily Mak, that there was no comprehensive and accurate reference guide for online music distribution and the legalities behind it. As practicing attorneys with some background in academia (Cecily as an adjunct at the UC Hastings College of the Law, and Allen as full time professor at Berklee College of Music), we saw the need for a guide for our students as well. Many things have changed since the release of the first edition in 2009, and as a result, I have continued to revise this book to help direct and support colleagues, students, and anyone interested in the music industry through the muddy waters of the convergence of technology and music.

Formidable outside forces, such as the birth of a new technology, can forever alter arts and culture in our world. The advent of the Internet and the MP3, as well as digital recording technology, caused a dramatic paradigm shift in the control and delivery of creative assets that is still being defined. Entire catalogs of content are now traded more quickly than a register could ring up a sale at a record store. Digital sales are now shrinking while streams of music continue to grow exponentially, and tools for distribution and consumption change consistently. People are living more and more of their lives in the metaverse. Gaps in copyright (the law that protects artistic works and allows creators to control the exploitation of their works) continue to emerge, and courts are left to apply decades-old law to unanticipated situations. New legislation is often introduced around the world, but as stakeholders lobby to maintain the status quo, rarely does significant change occur. (The 2018 Music Modernization Act, and 2019 EU Copyright Directive being exceptions, rather than the norm.)

On the other side of the debate, the "copyleft" movement seems to argue for the reduction of, or extinguishment, of copyright altogether for an alleged greater cultural good. Leaders of this movement point to remarkably creative works that are outright illegal due to the inclusion of unlicensed content, and there are entire genres of music and active creative "remix" communities whose work is stifled by the difficulty and costs associated with complying with current copyright law. Further, large technology companies who benefit from patent and IP protection on their own products make significant dollars using copyrighted content, causing a volatile debate about the "transfer of value."

On the business side of things, while online piracy still eats into recorded music revenues, legitimate digital streaming models have reached nearly full market penetration in some markets. However, while there is much debate about the future of the music industry, one thing remains clear: music consumption has never been higher. With music surrounding us in television, film, video games, satellite radio, and the ability to listen to more than fifty million songs in our pocket, we listen and consume more than ever. But, does this devalue music?

In the coming pages, you will learn the basics of copyright law and policy as it exists today, and how copyright applies to music. We'll look at the revenue sources for both songwriters and artists, and examine the different models for digital distribution. The appendixes provide reference resources. Hopefully, you'll walk away with an understanding of the basics of music and copyright in the digital age. By then, I may already be again rewriting this manuscript to include all of the changes in law, policy, and the industry that have taken place since the release of this third edition. This edition also includes three sample contracts, available online via the link provided on the first page of this book.

CHAPTER 1

History of the Music Industry and Copyright Law

When one thinks of the music industry, thoughts quickly turn to thrilling live performances, gripping albums, and creative marketing techniques, not tediously negotiated contracts or large-scale litigation. However, few industries are as reliant upon compliance with applicable law (including contracts) to derive income as the recorded music industry. The emergence of the original Napster in the late 1990s shone a glaring spotlight on the industry's dependence on lawful distribution models. It was via this end-user revolution that millions of consumers became adept at circumventing long-established distribution methods and long standing copyright laws. (*Copyright* is the right of an owner of a creative work to control the uses of the work and financially benefit from its exploitation. It initially vests in the author of the work, but may be later transferred.) As we continue to evolve in today's evermore-networked world, the application and enforcement of current copyright law becomes increasingly critical to the evolution and strength of the entire music and entertainment industry.

MUSIC FORMATS

Recorded music has a long history of distribution via a variety of changing formats and media. In the 1870s, the cylinder emerged as the first recording technology. Thomas Edison then captured the first recorded human voice in 1877 and was issued a patent for his recording technique that same year. The infant record industry began shortly thereafter with the proliferation of device manufacturers and music promoters. By the turn of the century, record labels were springing up, and music as a business began to flourish. In 1913, flat discs started to outgrow cylinders as media for recorded music, and in 1914, ASCAP (the American Society of Composers, Authors and Publishers) was founded to collect public performance fees under the newly enacted 1909 copyright law. Sales of prerecorded music grew quickly in parallel; in fact, sales revenues were over $1.4 billion in 1921, using 2021 dollars.

FIG. 1.1. Wax Cylinders. Edison Records made black wax cylinders.

The cylinder was quickly followed by the gramophone as a popular tool for playing recorded music. The Victrola gramophone was released in 1906, and in 1930, the Gramophone Company and the Columbia Graphophone Company merged to become Electrical and Musical Industries (EMI), which was one of the four remaining major label distributors for recorded music until its breakup and sale to Warner and Sony in 2012. The year 1903 brought the first release of prerecorded music on disc records on the Monarch Record Label.

The development of radio, at around the same time as the emergence of recorded music, served to promote the listening of music, and it brought that music directly into people's homes from distant places. Initially a two-way communications tool for the military and marine navigation, radio was born in the late 1800s and early 1900s, but did not emerge as a commercial product until the 1920s. In 1895, scientists Guglielmo Marconi, Heinrich Hertz, and Alexander Popov conducted experiments and demonstrations of communication through wireless devices. In 1906, Reginald Fessenden in Massachusetts made the first audio radio broadcast ever, including himself playing the violin and reading the Bible. With all of these changes afoot, no longer was music something seen only live, but rather a portable and transmittable commodity.

At first, radio was seen as a competitor to the recorded music industry. Similar to the recent decline in sales resulting from the distribution of music over the Internet, in the early days of radio, recorded music sales fell rapidly and experts predicted the demise of the then bustling recorded music industry, as people substituted listening to the radio for the purchase of recorded music. As Stan Liebowitz noted in his 2004 study of the impact of radio on recorded music:

> *The recording industry underwent a devastating decline shortly after the advent of radio. Even some commentators who assign the cause of the recording industry's decline to radio's emergence believe that the major impact of radio on record sales changed from substitution to exposure, and that radio now enhances sales of recordings.*[1]

Many analysts believe that the fall in record sales, from $75 million in 1929 to $26 million in 1938 (with a low point of $5 million in 1933) was partially due to the introduction of radio, although we must assume sales were also affected by the economic stresses associated with the Great Depression. In the end, however, radio's ability to introduce the public to new music made it become one of the greatest marketing tools for the sale of recorded music, not a competitor.

---

1 Liebowitz, Stan J. "The Elusive Symbiosis: The Impact of Radio on the Record Industry." *Review of Economic Research on Copyright Issues.* 1: (2004), 93–118.

Some compare the decline in record sales following the introduction of radio with the recent fall due to the availability of music for free online. However, we can differentiate the two phenomena based on their relative substitutive natures. While radio "request" shows became common in the 1950s, with listeners calling stations and requesting songs, the requested song was not always played, and if it was, rarely was it played immediately. Conversely, the availability of songs for illegal download on the Internet does substitute for the purchase and immediate consumption of recorded music, since potential consumers can immediately fulfill a desire for a certain song. Liebowitz noted that:

> *The substitution effect, at first blush, seems likely to be stronger in the case of MP3 downloads than for radio play of music due to the fact that downloads provide the listener with a copy of the song that has virtually identical attributes to the purchased version. There would seem to be little reason to purchase the song under these circumstances, leading to a very strong substitution effect. Listening to the radio does not leave the listener with a useable alternative that can substitute for the purchase of prerecorded music.*[2]

So while the radio and the new songs it could bring to the home initially captivated listeners, it ultimately could not satisfy consumers' demand for specific music. Radio today is now less promotional, since music is "accessed" rather than sold. This becomes important when we begin to discuss payment to rights holders for radio play.

Other media for recorded music developed over time, with the introduction by Columbia of 33-rpm 12-inch discs in 1948, and the release of stereo LPs in the late 1950s. Within the 1960s, audiocassettes, eight-track cartridges, and Dolby noise reduction all entered the fray as well. By the late 1970s, the leap to digital was underway, largely led by Philips, and in 1979 Philips and Sony Technology teamed up to design the new digital audio disc.[3] A task force, led by Kees Immink and Toshitad Doi, progressed the research into laser technology and optical discs that had been started by Philips in 1977.[4] Philips and Sony eventually agreed on a standard sampling rate of 44.1 kHz and 16-bit audio, and the disc ended up with a 12 cm diameter due to Sony's insistence that a disc hold all of Beethoven's 9th symphony, which clocked in at 74 minutes. The CD ultimately had its first commercial

---

2   Liebowitz, Stan J. "The Elusive Symbiosis: The Impact of Radio on the Record Industry." *Review of Economic Research on Copyright Issues*. 1: (2004)

3   Pohlmann, Ken C., *The Compact Disc Handbook*, 2nd Edition, A-R Editions Inc., 1992.

4   news.bbc.co.uk, "How the CD was Developed," August 2007.

release in Germany in 1982 with ABBA's *The Visitors*.

Despite initial opposition by U.S. record labels who thought the format would confuse customers and ruin the business, CDs eventually became the standard media for recorded music, with their full digital sound and no loss of frequencies or tape hiss. Labels began to gorge themselves on added revenue, which resulted from consumers' replacement of their recorded music libraries with the CD format, and in 2000, global CD sales peaked at 2.455 billion units.

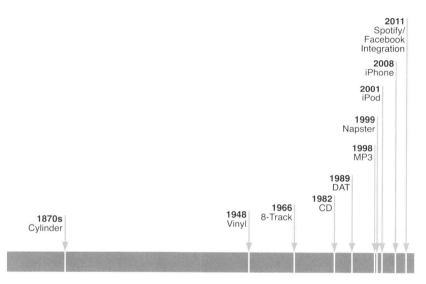

FIG. 1.2. Timeline of Recording Media

In 1989, Sony released Digital Audio Tape (DAT) technology. Despite the fact that DAT never took off as a widely used consumer medium, it was immensely important in the development of recorded music distribution, because it was the first technology to allow re-recording of music multiple times without significant loss of sound quality. Not surprisingly, its debut as a consumer product touched off a firestorm of piracy concerns, and despite the fact that Sony was unable to build DAT into a widely used format, the technology ultimately resulted in the passage of the Audio Home Recording Act of 1992 in the U.S. We will discuss the Act in chapter 2.

A Game Changer

A transformation began with the development and emergence of the commercial Internet in the 1990s, which, with its new high-speed broadband capabilities, brought the ability to send and share large data files quickly and easily. Nearly simultaneously, the German company Fraunhofer-Gesellschaft developed MP3 technology, which allowed for the compression of audio files into manageable sizes. MP3s use a lossy compression algorithm designed to greatly reduce the amount of data required to represent the audio recording and yet maintain the sound of a faithful reproduction. It works by reducing the accuracy of certain parts of sound that are deemed beyond the auditory resolution ability of most people, resulting in a file that is 8 to 10 percent of the size of the CD file created from the original audio source. All developers of MP3 encoders and decoders/players now pay a licensing fee to Fraunhofer.

FIG. 1.3. The Portable MP3 File. MP3 files are widely compatible and easily transferred.

The public quickly realized that a digital copy of a song in MP3 format, at about 3 to 5 megabytes in size, could easily be shared over data lines. A song could now be sent via the Internet in as little as one minute, and sites emerged such as MP3.com, which allowed independent bands to post and share music. (MP3.com later became one of the first targets of music industry lawsuits, which alleged the site was making copyrighted material available for free.)

FIG. 1.4. Fiber Optic Cables. Fiber optic cables began bringing broadband access to life in the 1990s.

Free-for-All?

In 1999, Shawn Fanning, then a student at Northeastern University in Boston, developed a computer program called Napster, which took advantage of the combination of MP3 and broadband technologies to allow "peer-to-peer" (P2P) file sharing. Via a simple search interface, Napster enabled users to search for and share files across the Internet, and music, newly encoded as MP3s, became easily traded. Fanning testified in a congressional hearing of his idea:

> *I began designing and programming a real-time system for locating MP3 files of other users on the Internet. I designed the Napster software to find MP3s because they are the most compressed format (in consideration of bandwidth) and they were very popular at the time.*

However, unlike MP3.com, which provided files from its central server, Napster merely provided a search service—a central database that connected users with other users who were online and "sharing" their MP3 files. The files went directly from one user's computer to another, bypassing any Napster equipment. The program's popularity grew phenomenally fast, and users shared over 1.7 billion songs in November of 2000.

Thus, a mere consumer, rather than a music or technology company, became the designer of the next wave of the music industry, and broadband Internet access, MP3 technology, and Fanning's computer program converged to create an easy way to share music files without any requirement of payment for the copyrighted material. Record sales were immediately impacted, with sales declining over a half billion dollars in 2000.

The Recording Industry Association of America (RIAA), which represents the interests of major and independent record labels, sued Fanning and Napster in 2000 for contributory copyright infringement, contributing the then-current statutorily allowed maximum $100,000 in damages for each copyrighted song that had been traded on the service, which equaled hundreds of millions of dollars. Napster argued that because the files were never on Napster's servers, and they merely provided an interface enabling direct connections between users, they were not infringing on any intellectual property and that their service should fall under the safe harbor protections of the Digital Millennium Copyright Act (the "DMCA"), which protects Internet service providers (and some other services) from liability. Napster lost the original ruling in the summer of 2000, but continued to operate pending an appeal. However, the appeals court in San Francisco issued an injunction in February of 2001 that required Napster to stop allowing the sharing of copyrighted material. (We will analyze the Napster ruling in more detail in chapter 11.)

Because Napster did not have a mechanism to effectively filter out copyrighted material from other authorized works, the injunction essentially forced the complete shutdown of the company. However, other peer-to-peer sharing services such as Kazaa and Morpheus appeared and took its place, and the music industry had been forever altered. Karl Greenfeld noted in *Time Magazine* that:

Love it or hate it, that's what Napster has done: changed the world. It has forced record companies to rethink their business models and record-company lawyers and recording artists to defend their intellectual property. It has forced purveyors of "content," like Time Warner, parent company of Time Magazine, *to wonder what content will even be in the near future. Napster and Fanning have come to personify the bloody intersection where commerce, culture, and the First Amendment are colliding. On behalf of five media companies, the Recording Industry Association of America (RIAA) has sued Napster, claiming the website and Fanning's program are facilitating the theft of intellectual property. Most likely the blueprint for the future of the entertainment industry will be drawn from this ruling.*[5]

Though labels were successful in their fight against Napster, attempts to close individual file sharing sites through litigation were costly and seemed fruitless, with new services emerging continuously. In the summer of 2003, the RIAA began a different enforcement effort: targeting individuals who traded music online with civil lawsuits. Relying on the DMCA to issue subpoenas to Internet service providers forcing them to divulge the identities of certain users, the association, in a very high profile attempt to threaten and scare consumers engaged in illicit downloading, directly sued individuals who had downloaded pirated music online. Between 2003 and the summer of 2008, when the RIAA publicly announced it would stop suing, the group sued approximately 30,000 downloaders, seeking statutory damages up to $150,000 per violation. Some alleged offenders chose to settle, for an average of about $12,000, and others fought vigorously in court. (In August of 2008, the RIAA publicly announced a change in strategy, stating that they would no longer sue individuals for file sharing, but rather work with Internet service providers (ISPs) to try to stop online piracy through a variety of other initiatives.)

---

5 Greenfeld, Karl Taro. "Meet the Napster. Shawn Fanning was 18 when he wrote the code that changed the world. His fate, and ours, is now in the court's hands." *Time Magazine.* 2 October 2000.

THE RECORDING INDUSTRY ASSOCIATION OF AMERICA

The Recording Industry Association of America (RIAA) was formed in 1952, with the initial purpose of administering the RIAA equalization curve, a standard of frequency response applied to vinyl records during manufacturing and playback.

However, the RIAA is now one of the largest lobbying groups in the U.S., with 1,600 member labels doing over $7 billion in sales revenue in 2014. Its members account for nearly 90 percent of recorded music sold in the United States. While the RIAA has continued to participate in creating and administering technical standards for systems of music recording and reproduction, they also seek to influence legislation on copyright and protect the interests of their member labels. The RIAA has been involved in numerous lawsuits against infringers for the downloading of music, as well as actions such as the suit against Rio alleging that its MP3 player in the late 1990s violated the Audio Home Recording Act.

The RIAA is also responsible for certifying album sales as gold (500,000 units), platinum (1,000,000 units), and diamond (10,000,000 units). Other awards are available for certain levels of single and digital sales, and now for streaming as well, where 1,500 streams equals 10 track sales which equal one album sale.[6]

The failure of the recording industry to proactively respond to the development of new technologies, and its aggressive stance in targeting both Web services and individuals, can be credited with causing a social response that presumes piracy to be acceptable. The public, many of whom in the past felt that CD prices were too high, saw record companies suing grandmothers and children for downloading music, which resulted in a public relations nightmare for labels. As a result, many consumers responded by believing piracy was okay because labels were the "big corporate enemy." As a result, the new generation of today's music consumers—even some musicians who actually stand to lose income from online piracy—has been indifferent to the labels' woes.

---

6   www.riaa.com/riaa-debuts-album-award-streams/

As all of these new technologies emerged, the recording industry fell far behind in implementing new offerings that could provide music to consumers via new formats and monetize their intellectual property assets. While technology and device companies continued the development of new products to download, store, and transport music, labels instead focused their efforts (and money) on litigation. In the fall of 2001, Apple Computer released its first iPod, a music player capable of storing five gigabytes of data, or roughly one thousand songs in MP3 format. Early adopters of the iPod realized they now had a device enabling the easy portability of digital music, including music in a digital format "ripped" from compact discs, and digital music grew quickly as a distribution format. Unfortunately for record labels, those gains came primarily as pirated material traded on peer-to-peer networks. By 2003, record labels and copyright owners realized that digital music had reached a critical mass, despite their resistance to the format and the lack of a viable option for online music sales.

As they found themselves behind the times and figurative eight ball, record company executives finally listened and acquiesced when Steve Jobs, CEO of Apple, approached them about a paid download store, where consumers could purchase single tracks of music that could be transferred to the iPod and played on up to five computers, with their playback limited by means of Apple's FairPlay digital rights management (DRM) technology. Apple rolled out the iTunes Music Store in April of 2003, a full four years after Napster's introduction, and initially offered over 200,000 tracks from the five major record labels at the time. The rapid adoption of the digital delivery of music, which happened almost completely without the permission and/or backing of music labels, had essentially forced record label executives to license their music to Apple for sale under a paid download scheme, since the alternative was the continued loss of revenue to digital piracy. While DRM was initially a major selling point to get the record labels to sell their catalogs on the iTunes store, Apple and most other large online music retailers have now made music available for purchase without built-in playback or copying protection or other restriction mechanisms.

WHAT IS "DRM"?

DRM, or digital rights management, is a mechanism included in files to ensure that the files cannot be shared beyond the initial permissions granted by the provider of the file (among other capabilities). In Apple's case with FairPlay, a song could only be authorized to play on five computers. Attempts to play the song on other computers would require a user to enter a password to access the file. Separately, DRM now enables systems such as Tidal or Spotify to tether downloads to subscriptions, by requiring the player to be connected monthly to confirm a subscription is valid. If a user has cancelled his or her subscription, DRM disables the downloaded files.

More recently, on-demand music services, ranging from YouTube (the world's largest online music destination) to Spotify have begun to dominate the marketplace, years after predictions from executives and researchers that subscription-based services might increase recorded music revenue to above that of the late 1990s, before the industry was struck by Napster and the ensuing widespread piracy. Much of Spotify's popularity in the U.S. originated from its integration with Facebook, allowing users to show their friends via the Facebook feed what music they are listening to via the service. This social aspect gave subscription models something they had been lacking for years: widespread public awareness. Spotify, as of 2021, boasts 150m+ monthly average users, with Apple Music's offering barely trailing behind, since Apple's foray into the marketplace was delayed and likely only a result of its download business shifting to other platforms.

Sweden, the home of Spotify, is widely seen as a model for the digital music business, with dramatic decreases in piracy in recent years, and with digital accounting for 90 percent of music revenue, and more than 70 percent coming from subscription revenue.

WHY IS COPYRIGHT IMPORTANT TO MUSIC?

The foregoing brief history of the music business illustrates the importance of copyright law to the music industry. Copyright is the right of a creator to control various uses and distributions of his or her creations. It is copyright that protects the music created and the creator's right to make money from such music. *Without copyright, there would be no recorded music industry.*

Copyright was initially conceived to protect authors and developers of creative works from having their works misappro-priated and to provide them with a source of revenue, which would hopefully spur creativity. Modern copyright law has its origins in British stationers' attempts to protect works from piracy through the passage of the Statute of Anne in 1710, which gave the monopoly control over a work back to the author instead of a publisher. In an effort to encourage creativity, the United States Congress enacted the first copyright legislation in the United States in 1790 to provide a mechanism for protection and reward for authors and creators of artistic works. This first law protected maps, charts, and books for a period of fourteen years, with fourteen-year renewals.

Anno Octavo

Annæ Reginæ.

An Act for the Encouragement of Learning, by Vesting the Copies of Printed Books in the Authors or Purchasers of such Copies, during the Times therein mentioned.

Whereas Printers, Booksellers, and other Persons have of late frequently taken the Liberty of Printing, Reprinting, and Publishing, or causing to be Printed, Reprinted, and Published Books, and other Writings, without the Consent of the Authors or Proprietors of such Books and Writings, to their very great Detriment, and too often to the Ruin of them and their Families : For Preventing therefore such Practices for the future, and for the Encouragement of Learned Men to Compose and Write useful Books ; May it please Your Majesty, that it may be Enacted, and be it Enacted by the Queens most Excellent Majesty, by and with the Advice and Consent of the Lords Spiritual and Temporal, and Commons in this present Parliament Assembled, and by the Authority of the same, That from and after the Tenth Day of April, One thousand seven hundred and ten, the Author of any Book or Books already Printed, who hath not Transferred to any other the Copy or Copies of such Book or Books, Share or Shares thereof, or the Bookseller or Booksellers, Printer or Printers, or other Person or Persons, who hath or have Purchased or Acquired the Copy or Copies of any Book or Books, in order to Print or Reprint the same, shall have the sole Right and Liberty of Printing such Book and Books for the Term of One and twenty Years, to Commence from the said Tenth Day of April, and no longer ; and that the Author of any Book or Books already Composed and not Printed and Published, or that shall hereafter be Composed, and his Assignee, or Assigns, shall have the sole Liberty of Printing and Reprinting such Book and Books for the Term of Four-

6   Tt 2   teen

FIG. 1.5. The Statute of Anne

U.S. copyright law was strengthened in 1909, extending the term of copyright to twenty-eight years, with twenty-eight year renewals. The 1909 Act also expanded the list of protected works, and for the first time, introduced the concept of a compulsory license for musical works, which is a key part of the foundation of today's music industry. However, sound recordings did not officially qualify for copyright protection under federal law until 1972. They had previously been protected, if at all, under state law.

In 1976, Congress completely rewrote the United States Copyright Act, which came into effect on January 1, 1978, and that law forms the basis for authors, musicians, and other creators to derive income from their works today in the U.S.

CHAPTER 2

Copyright Law Basics

The development of copyright law has been largely reactive. It has evolved from its earlier renditions in response to changing industry and intellectual property rights demands. The law can be traced back to Congress's power in the Constitution "to promote the Progress of Science and useful Arts, by securing for limited times to Authors and Inventors the exclusive Right to their Writings and Discoveries." [1] For example, as mentioned earlier, the development of radio brought concern to copyright owners that the provision of free music would provide them no gain and instead diminish the value of their intellectual property. However, unlike the technologies of today, copyright owners found that then existing copyright law already protected their rights, and the new technology led to the development of new methods for collecting revenue.

TWO COPYRIGHTS

There are *two* copyrights vital to the music business, protecting every recorded song:

1. The copyright in the *musical composition* (song)—the lyrics and music; and
2. The copyright in the *sound recording*—the actual recorded performance of a particular musical composition.

---

1 *United States Constitution*, Article 1, Section 8

Artistic works in the United States today are protected under the Copyright Act of 1976, with various amendments. Specifically, the law protects:

> ...works of authorship fixed in any tangible medium of expression, now known or later developed, from which they can be perceived, reproduced, or otherwise communicated, either directly or with the aid of a machine or device...

—Copyright Act of 1976, 17 U.S.C. § 102

This means that a work must be written down, recorded, or somehow preserved outside the brain of its creator in order for copyright protection to apply. This was a change from earlier laws that required actual publication of the work for the copyright to vest—to become legally yours.

The Copyright Act lists eight categories of works to be covered, although the list is not meant to be all encompassing:

1. literary works;
2. musical works, including any accompanying words;
3. dramatic works, including any accompanying music;
4. pantomimes and choreographic works;
5. pictorial, graphic, and sculptural works;
6. motion pictures and other audiovisual works;
7. sound recordings; and
8. architectural works.

—Copyright Act of 1976, 17 U.S.C. § 102

We must note that copyright *does not* protect ideas or concepts (which may be protected by patent law), but rather the *expressions* of ideas or concepts. For example, copyright law protects the layout of a version of the yellow pages, but not the phone numbers and addresses included. Specific to music, Bob Dylan's lyrics and melody to the song "Hurricane" are covered, while the idea of a wrongly imprisoned man is not.

COPYRIGHT'S SIX EXCLUSIVE RIGHTS

1. Reproduction
2. The preparation of derivative works
3. Distribution
4. Public performance
5. Public display
6. Public performance of a sound recording in non-exempt digital formats

Copyright law in the United States provides a copyright owner of a protected work with six exclusive rights in that work:

1. To reproduce the copyrighted work in copies or phonorecords;

2. To prepare derivative works based upon the copyrighted work;

3. To distribute copies or phonorecords of the copyrighted work to the public by sale or other transfer of ownership, or by rental, lease, or lending;

4. In the case of literary, musical, dramatic, and choreographic works, pantomimes, and motion pictures and other audiovisual works, to perform the copyrighted work publicly;

5. In the case of literary, musical, dramatic, and choreographic works, pantomimes, and pictorial, graphic, or sculptural works, including the individual images of a motion picture or other audiovisual work, to display the copyrighted work publicly; and

6. In the case of sound recordings, to perform the copyrighted work publicly by means of a digital audio transmission.

—Copyright Act of 1976, 17 U.S.C. § 106

The first of these rights, "the right to reproduce the work," means that copyright owners can control the copying of their works. They have the exclusive right to make copies, or to prevent others from copying their works. This could encompass everything from the duplication of an album or sheet music to the use of a song lyric in another musical work.

The second exclusive right, "the right to prepare derivative works," is similar to the right to prevent copies from being made. In this case, a copyright owner can prevent all others from making derivative works that are based on the original work (or "loose copies" of the original work). Copyright law defines a derivative work as follows:

> ...a work based upon one or more preexisting works, such as a translation, musical arrangement, drama-tization, fictionalization, motion picture version, sound recording, art reproduction, abridgment, condensation, or any other form in which a work may be recast, transformed, or adapted. A work consisting of editorial revisions, annotations, elaborations, or other modifications which, as a whole, represent an original work of authorship, is a "derivative work."

—Copyright Act of 1976, 17 U.S.C. § 101

CAN YOU BORROW A RIFF?

Question: A young guitarist loves Slash and the Guns N' Roses song "Sweet Child O' Mine." He "borrows" the main riff from the song and the chorus, and includes them in a new song he writes.
    Can he legally do this?

Answer: *No. Guns N' Roses, as the writer of the song (or their assignee), controls the right to prevent others from using part of their song to create another work. Not only does copyright law allow Guns N' Roses to prevent copying of their work, the young guitarist's song could be considered a derivative work under copyright law, and Guns N' Roses has the right to control such adaptations of their work.*

The third right, "to distribute copies or phonorecords of the copyrighted work," reserves the right of distribution to a copyright holder—the creator of the music—unless he transfers that right to someone else. The restriction takes the exclusive right to copy to a different level, meaning a band can authorize unlimited copies of their most recent single to be pressed, but can still control where and how those copies are provided to the public. For example, they may choose not to allow online distribution of their single. This exclusive right becomes increasingly important as distribution methods evolve, and we'll discuss it more later in the book as we move into our analysis of online delivery of music.

The fourth right, "to publicly perform" a work, is of special concern in the music industry. The right essentially permits a copyright holder to control performances in public of a creative work. Such "public performances" include the "performance" of a composition via an on-demand stream rendered over the Internet. The right does not extend to sound recordings in the U.S. (an exception is made for digital performances, which we address in a moment), but covers musical composition copyrights. (This means that artists are not paid when their song is played on AM/FM radio, but writers/musical compositions copyright holders are.) It is the public performance right that led to the development of performing rights organizations (PROs), which are responsible for collecting revenues from television and radio broadcasters and live music venues, as well as digital services, and then distributing the monies to their member writers and publishers. The PROs for musical works—in the U.S., the American Society of Composers, Authors and Publishers (ASCAP), Broadcast Music, Inc. (BMI), and the Society of European Stage Authors and Composers (SESAC)—pay their writers and publishers based on complicated formulas that track airplay and determine how much the writers (and/ or copyright owners, as the case may be) of a musical composition should be paid for the public performances of their song. More recently, new PROs such as Global Music Rights and Kobalt's AMRA have announced plans to offer writers an alternative for the collection of digital performance royalties on a global basis.

PERFORMANCE RIGHTS ORGANIZATIONS

Collective licensing organizations exist in most developed countries. In the U.S., ASCAP, BMI, and SESAC compete to sign writers (see Appendix B for contact information). In most other countries, a single, government-controlled collecting society exists to collect public performance royalties for copyright holders. Interestingly enough, in nearly every other developed country, sound recording copyright holders are also eligible to exercise public performance rights in their copyrights and receive income from analog transmissions of their works (such as traditional AM and FM radio).

Some foreign societies include:

- Canada: Society of Composers, Authors and Music Publishers of Canada <www.socan.ca>
- France: Société des Auteurs, Compositeurs et Éditeurs de Musique <www.sacem.fr>
- Italy: Società Italiana degli Autori ed Editori <www.siae.it>
- Japan: Japanese Society for Rights of Authors, Composers and Publishers <www.jasrac.or.jp>
- Spain: Sociedad General de Autores y Editores <www.sgae.es>
- The Netherlands: Buma/Stemra <www.bumastemra.nl>
- U.K.: PRS for Music, previously known as Performing Rights Society (PRS): <www.prsformusic.com>

The fifth right, "to publicly display" a work, is not of as much concern for the music industry. It is, however, an important right for visual artists such as painters. For musicians, from a logistical perspective, the right applies only to musical works because "sound recordings" cannot by their nature be displayed. An inference can be drawn that the only protection, therefore, for music under this right is the right to control the public exhibition of lyrics and music notes to a musical work. Music is generally protected by the right to publicly perform a work, as discussed above.

The sixth right, "of public performance for sound recordings in digital transmissions," was added to copyright law by Congress with the passage of the Digital Performance Right in Sound Recordings Act of 1995 (the DPRSRA). (We will discuss the history of DPRSRA and its ramifications in more detail in chapter 3.) As we mentioned earlier, sound recordings do not currently fall under the fourth exclusive right of copyright holders (public performance), although musical compositions do. Again, this means that artists or record labels or whoever controls the copyright in a sound recording (the "recorded performance" of a certain song) do not receive public performance income for airplay on terrestrial radio. However, with the passage of the DPRSRA, copyright owners of sound recordings have the right to collect royalties for the public performance of their works through digital means, like satellite radio or streaming services. Digital radio or "webcasting" licenses are granted pursuant to a compulsory license administered by a government-sanctioned arm of the RIAA, SoundExchange. On-demand streaming licenses are voluntary and are negotiated with each sound recording copyright holder individually.

WHO PAYS RADIO ROYALTIES?

Question: A band, Wanton Success, records an original song and releases it as a single to terrestrial radio, satellite radio, and digital radio stations who stream the song to online listeners. From whom should Wanton Success expect to receive public performance royalty payments for the song?

Answer: *Satellite radio will be required to compensate Wanton Success for airplay of their song as both the writers and the performers. Terrestrial (AM/FM) radio in the U.S. will not be required to pay for the public performance of the **sound recording** but will be required to pay public performance royalties to the band as the writers of the **composition**. Any terrestrial radio station that also streams their station online (or any other online broadcaster) will also be required to make royalty payments to the band for the public performance of the sound recording via streaming to SoundExchange and the musical composition to the PROs.*

DURATION OF COPYRIGHT

Copyright has a limited duration during which the owner can exercise his or her exclusive rights. Any works created after January 1, 1978 are protected for a period of the life of the creator plus 70 years. This means that if you create a work, copyright will last throughout your lifetime and your heirs or other owners of the copyright will be entitled to enforce the copyright in the work for 70 years from the date of your death. Anonymous works (or works created under a pseudonym) and works for hire have protection for 95 years from the date of first publication, or 120 years from the date of creation, whichever expires first. [2]

LENGTH OF COPYRIGHT PROTECTION

Date of Creation	Copyright Term
Prior to January 1, 1978 but not expiring before December 31, 2002	28 years + 67-year renewal term
Prior to January 1, 1978 but set to expire before December 31, 2002	Will not expire before 12/31/2047
After January 1, 1978	Life of the author + 70 years

Copyright duration becomes more complicated for those works created before January 1, 1978. Any work created prior to January 1, 1978 in which copyright would not have expired before December 31, 2002, is entitled to an initial term of protection of 28 years, with the right of renewal for an additional 67 years. Works created prior to January 1, 1978 but which would have expired before December 31, 2002 now will continue to have copyright protection until at least December 31, 2047. (The "Sonny Bono Copyright Extension Act," passed in 1998, extended the term of copyright by 20 years. The Act was widely known as the "Mickey Mouse Extension Act," as it was fought for by entertainment companies who didn't want to lose protection for their older assets and effectively granted Disney additional protection for the Mickey Mouse character.)

---

2   *Copyright Act of 1976*, 17 U.S.C. § 302

COPYRIGHT DURATION OF WORKS FOR HIRE

Works for hire are protected for a different period of time than works in which copyright vests in the original author. Protection lasts for 95 years from the date of first publication, or 120 years from the date of creation, whichever comes first.

When copyright protection ends for a creative work, it is said to have fallen into the "public domain." A work in the public domain may be used by any person for any purpose, including the creation of derivative works, without restriction or payment to the original author. Many old church hymns, the national anthem, and older "campfire songs" all became public domain many years ago. Further, new arrangements of public domain works (e.g., adding lyrics to a Beethoven piano concerto) are subject to new copyright protection with the same rights and protections as works not created from public domain source material.

TRANSFERRING COPYRIGHT

Any of the six exclusive rights of a copyright owner, or all of them together, may be given or sold to a third party. Four types of transfers exist for copyrighted works:

1. Assignment

2. Exclusive License

3. Non-Exclusive License

4. Work for Hire

A copyright owner may grant limited rights in a work to a third party for a specified period of time or in perpetuity (license). Alternatively, a copyright owner may assign his or her entire copyright to another party, meaning the owner no longer has any rights to the work (assignment).[3] (Such a transfer must be in writing signed by the owner of the rights conveyed.) For example, in a publishing deal, a songwriter may assign all or part of the copyright in his or her song to a publisher in exchange for an advance of royalties and the opportunity to have the publisher place the song on other artists' albums or in film and television. Separately, an artist might license his or her sound recordings to a

---

3 *Copyright Act of 1976,* 17 U.S.C. § 201(d)

record label for a period of time, during which the label will try to profit from distributing the recordings.

Under a *license*, the licensee's right to the copyright can be for some or all of the rights under the copyright and will terminate upon expiration of the license term, returning the rights to the copyright owner. In comparison, under an *assignment*, the acquirer of the rights maintains the rights until the copyright expires, with one caveat: Under U.S. copyright law, an assignor of rights is entitled to terminate the assignment during the five-year period beginning in the 36th year after the transfer of right.[4] (The period is during the five years after the first fifty-six years, or January 1, 1978, whichever comes first, for works created before January 1, 1978.) So, in the example above, the songwriter could terminate the assignment of his or her copyright to the publisher after thirty-five years and regain ownership of the song. Recent court cases have held that this right to a termination of transfer *cannot be waived* contractually in the initial sale agreement.[5]

Finally, there also exists in copyright law the concept of a *work for hire*. A work for hire is a creative work that is deemed to have been commissioned specially by an employer, and the employer will be deemed the author and own the copyright from the work's inception (as opposed to the case of an assignment, in which case the copyright is deemed to have vested in the creator upon creation, and the rights are later assigned or given to someone else). There need not be, however, an employer-employee relationship between the creator and the person commissioning the work for hire; a contract stipulating that the work is to be a work for hire upon its inception will suffice as long it fits into the legislated categories.

The Copyright Act specifically defines "work for hire" as:

    (1) a work prepared by an employee within the
    scope of his or her employment, or

    (2) a work specially ordered or commissioned for
    use as a contribution to a collective work, as
    a part of a motion picture or other audiovisual
    work, as a sound recording, as a translation, as
    a supplementary work, as a compilation, as an
    instructional text, as a test, as answer mate-
    rial for a test, or as an atlas, if the parties

---

4   *Copyright Act of 1976*, 17 U.S.C. § 203(a)(3)

5   *Marvel Characters, Inc. v. Simon, F3d* ____, 2002 WL 31478878 (2d Cir. November 7, 2002)

> expressly agree in a written instrument signed
> by them that the work shall be considered a work
> made for hire.

> —*Copyright Act of 1976, 17 U.S.C. § 101*

Because the copyright with a work for hire vests in the employer and not the creator at the moment the work is created, there is no right to termination of transfer. The distinction becomes important as we talk about recording agreements. A recording agreement that states that the creator will assign the works (i.e., master recording) to a music company will allow the creator to regain copyright ownership in those works after thirty-five years, whereas an artist whose master recording is deemed a work for hire will never regain those rights, because he or she never had them to start. (Note that sound recordings cannot be works for hire by contract because they are not one of the specially delineated categories; therefore, the only time a sound recording is a work for hire is when the recording artist is actually an employee of the record label.) Musical compositions *can be* works for hire under contract, and many film scores are written as works for hire so that the movie studio does not have to worry about royalty payments or a reversion of the copyright interest in the song.

TERMINATION OF TRANSFER

As we saw earlier, all rights in a copyright will return to the owner automatically at the end of a limited term license. However, even if an author who assigns his copyright away "in perpetuity" has the option to later terminate the transfer to the third party. As of the writing of this edition, the first works under the Copyright Act of 1976 are beginning to be eligible for termination, and in recent years, notable records like Prince's "Purple Rain," Michael Jackson's "Thriller," and Madonna's "Like a Virgin" have become eligible for this right, meaning the authors (or heirs) will hold substantial contract renegotiation power with the labels who have owned the sound recordings for decades.

If an author wishes to terminate a transfer, he/she must serve notice to the other party of his/her intent to terminate the grant of rights. In the event a work has multiple authors, a majority of the authors who executed the transfer must request the termination of the transfer. Notice must be given at least two years prior to the date on which an author wishes the transfer to be effective, but not more than ten years in advance. And in general, termination of the grant may be effected at any time during a period of five years beginning at the end of thirty-five years from the date of execution of the grant; or, if the grant covers the right of publication of the work, the period begins at the end of thirty-five years from the date of publication of the work under the grant or at the end of forty years from the date of execution of the grant, whichever term ends earlier.[6] Remember that this right would not apply to a work for hire, because the employer is deemed to be the author.

RECLAIMING RIGHTS DUE TO A TRANSFER OF AGREEMENT

Question: Wanton Success signs a publishing agreement with XYZ Music, under which the band will assign the rights in the songs on their already complete *Album One* to XYZ and will write the songs for *Album Two* as works for hire.

Thirty-five years later, the band hears that they can "get their masters back" by notifying the label under the Termination of Transfer provision. Will they be entitled to all of their master recordings?

Answer: *No. The band would be entitled to terminate their assignment of rights in the songs on* Album One, *but because the songs on* Album Two *were written as "works for hire," the copyright vested immediately in XYZ and is not subject to the Termination of Transfer provision.*

---

6   *Copyright Act of 1976,* 17 U.S.C. § 203(a)(3)

FILING AND DEPOSIT REQUIREMENTS

Many people believe that a work must be registered in order to be protected under copyright law. Copyright law does require that all copyrighted works be deposited with the Library of Congress within three months of publication; ironically, this "requirement" is *not* a condition of copyright protection.

Separately, the Register of Copyrights offers an optional registration for copyrights, allowing a copyright holder to place a copy on file to provide *prima facie* evidence of copyright owner-ship.[7] (*Prima facie* evidence is evidence that, unless rebutted, is sufficient to prove a fact.) This means that a court will weigh the copyright registration as proof of ownership in any infringement action unless someone proves otherwise, and the date of registration can be used as proof of the date of creation. As with the deposit requirement for the Library of Congress, registration is not required for copyright to vest.

HOW TO REGISTER A COPYRIGHT

Forms for registration can be found at www.copyright.gov, and online filing is available. "Form PA" is used to file for musical composition copyright, while "Form SR" is applicable for the sound recording copyright. Depending on your specific case, you may be able to register your musical work and sound recording copyrights on a single "Form SR" (generally if the copyright ownership is the same for all musical compositions and sound recordings being registered). Separate filings may also be made for each copyright if you wish to have separate registrations or if ownership is different between works. Deposit with the Library of Congress is sufficient to fulfill the deposit requirements of the Copyright Office, but the registration forms and fees must still be paid. Fees as of 2021 are $45 for a single author online registration, $65 online otherwise, and $85 for paper registration. (Note that the Copyright Office has a history of changing policies and fees fairly often, so be sure to read the instructions for filing.)

---

7   *Copyright Act of 1976,* 17 U.S.C. § 407

Instead, copyright always vests in a created work at the time of creation, in either the creator or the employer or other assignee. Registration is a prerequisite to the filing of a lawsuit for infringement.

Rather than filing for a copyright registration, some people choose to use what is commonly referred to as the "poor man's copyright." By mailing a copy of a work to yourself, having the post office postmark the envelope, and then not opening the envelope, you may be able to show a date of creation of the work, which took place prior to the postmark. While it's better than nothing, it is certainly not as advantageous as a formal copyright registration.

The main point here is that having evidence to prove the date of creation, whether in the form of official registration, publication and distribution, witness testimony, a computer timestamp, or another proof, will help to prove your case in an infringement action.

SHOULD I COPYRIGHT MY WORK?

Many artists and writers often wonder if they should bother to "copyright" their work. However, copyright vests in their work the minute it is fixed in a tangible medium of expression. Most often, they are referring to the official registration process, which is optional. *Registration is only required if you want to sue someone else for copyright infringement. It does not affect whether you hold the rights in your work.*

HOW DO I REGISTER THE COPYRIGHT IN MY WORK?

Question: Wanton Success has finished recording their first full-length studio album, which consists of twelve songs they fully wrote. They want to register their copyrights in both the sound recordings and musical compositions. Can they file just one copyright registration form, or will they need to register each song individually?

Answer: *Because Wanton Success wrote all of the musical compositions jointly, they will be able to register the musical composition copyrights together with their sound recordings on a "Form SR" at a total charge of $65. (The $65 fee is for online filings with more than one author in 2021.)*

NOTICE

"Notice" is also no longer a requirement for copyright in the United States, meaning that copyright owners are not required to put any type of notification on copies of their work. Of course, you are always free to include it anyway, and we suggest including it on any mass-distributed copies, showing the year of creation and the owner, such as "© Allen Bargfrede, 2021. All Rights Reserved."

APPROPRIATE NOTICE FORMATS

Copyright notice is not required, but the appropriate format, if you do choose to include it on copies of your work, is © for visually perceptible works, along with the year of first publication of the work and the name of the copyright owner, and ℗ for sound recordings such as phonorecords, also along with the year of first publication of the work and the name of the copyright owner. As an example, this book is © Berklee Press, 2021.

The phrase "All Rights Reserved" can also be used, but does not hold much weight in the United States. Prior to 2000, the phrase was required by countries who were signatories to the Buenos Aires Convention (see chapter 11), but the requirement no longer exists. Today, it may help reserve what are called "moral rights" in some foreign countries ("moral rights" are not recognized in the U.S.), which generally provide a right of attribution to the work and the right to protect the "integrity of the work." Think of them as "brand protection" for a creator.

ENFORCING COPYRIGHTS

If someone infringes one or more of a copyright holder's exclusive rights—for example, by plagiarizing a song's lyrics or melody or illegally selling copies—copyright law has established a series of remedies available to the copyright owner if he or she sues and prevails in a court of law.

Those remedies include:

1. *Injunctive relief.*[8] Injunctive relief means that a court of law could issue a ruling to stop the infringement immediately, whether or not a trial is pending regarding the infringement. An injunction might prohibit the manufacture and sale of an item that is alleged to infringe upon the rights of a valid copyright holder. For example, a CD containing a song that is alleged to have copied lyrics from a prior musical work could be removed from store shelves under a court order. RealNetworks was granted an injunction against Streambox in 1999 stopping Streambox from distributing products that violated the DMCA, and the original Napster was essentially forced out of business by a 2001 injunction requiring the company to filter copyrighted material (because they didn't have the technology in place to do so).

2. *Impounding of infringing items.*[9] A court could also issue an order requiring police to impound all items that are infringing. Upon final judgment that the items do infringe the rights of a third party, the court also has the authority to order destruction of the infringing property. For example, New York City Police could raid a warehouse containing illegal copies of compact discs and impound them until a trial adjudicates the matter. In 2005, the Sixth Circuit court ordered all copies of the first album by Notorious B.I.G., entitled *Ready to Die*, impounded after the court found that the album contained an unlicensed sample of the Ohio Players 1972 song "Singing in the Morning."[10] Note that this remedy is obviously more difficult to apply in a digital content world, because those items by their non-physical nature cannot be impounded.

3. *Actual damages, plus profits made by the infringer from the infringing works.*[11] If an item is deemed to be infringing, a copyright holder is entitled to recover the actual damages suffered by him or her as a result of the infringement. He or she is also entitled to any profits of the infringer that are not taken into account as part of the actual damages. In the

---

8 *Copyright Act of 1976*, 17 U.S.C. § 502
9 *Copyright Act of 1976*, 17 U.S.C. § 503
10 *Bridgeport Music, Inc. v. Justin Combs Publishing, 507 F.3d 470*
11 *Copyright Act of 1976*, 17 U.S.C. § 504

Notorious B.I.G. case, the plaintiffs were awarded $733,378 in "compensatory damages" related to the profits from the infringing material.[12]

4. *Statutory damages*.[13] Copyright law also sets forth certain minimum damages that can be awarded to a copyright holder from an infringer (known as *statutory damages*). The copyright owner may elect prior to final judgment to receive an award of statutory damages in lieu of actual damages, which for each work infringed in the action shall be at least $750 but less than $30,000. If a copyright is deemed to have been infringed willfully, the amount can be up to $150,000 per work infringed, but if the court finds the infringer was not aware and had no reason to be aware of his or her infringement, the statutory damages may be reduced to as low as $200 per work. Again, in the Notorious B.I.G. case, the plaintiffs also received an award of $150,000, the statutory maximum.[14]

5. *Criminal penalties*: If the infringement was committed willfully for purposes of commercial gain, or by the reproduction of one or more copies of a phonorecord or other copyrighted work within a 180-day period, or by making a work available to the public via a computer network, the infringer may be punished under criminal penalties set forth in 18 U.S.C. § 2319. Several members of the aPOCALYPSE pRODUCTION cREW group online were sent to prison for criminal copyright infringement for operating a service online for the illicit sharing of music on private servers. (Although not in the U.S., and therefore not under U.S. law, founders of the offshore file sharing service, the Pirate Bay, were also sent to jail in Sweden for criminal copyright infringement. As of this writing, the U.S. is trying to extradite Kim Dot-Com, the founder of MegaUpload, to stand trial for criminal charges of infringement.)

---

12 *Bridgeport Music, Inc. v. Justin Combs Publishing, 507 F.3d 470*
13 *Copyright Act of 1976, 17 U.S.C. § 504*
14 *Bridgeport Music, Inc. v. Justin Combs Publishing, 507 F.3d 470*

Criminal penalties can include:

- Making copies of a copyrighted work for financial gain: a minimum of one year in jail, and the penalties are stepped up to five years if the total value exceeded $2,500.

- Making copies of a copyrighted work, including via electronic means: a penalty of a year, or three years if the offense includes works that have a total retail value of $2,500 or more.

- Making a copyrighted work available on a computer network: up to three years in prison, or up to five years if such actions were for commercial advantage or finan-cial gain.

- Specific to music: anyone who records a live performance, or transmits or distributes such a live music performance, can be punished by up to a five-year jail penalty for the first offense.

Infringement actions must, by law, be instituted within three years after a claim arose for civil penalties or within five years after a criminal cause of action arose.

WHAT SHOULD I DO IF I THINK SOMEONE IS INFRINGING MY COPYRIGHT?

Question: Wanton Success wrote a song five years ago, and now a band called the Copier has released a song that contains my exact lyrics, but they credit themselves with writing it. What should the band do to protect its rights?

Answer: *If Wanton Success believes someone has copied its work, or is otherwise infringing on its copyright, there are several steps it should take:*

1. Send a "cease and desist letter." Such a letter informs or reminds the other party of the band's rights. A cease and desist letter typically demands removal of the infringing content from the market, and an accounting (detailed record of all sales or distributions) and fees for such uses (occasionally including attorneys' fees as well). Such a letter can also demand a license in the event that you just want to start collecting royalties for the use. This is generally the first step an attorney will take.

2. File a lawsuit. If the cease and desist letter doesn't work, the band will probably have to file a lawsuit against the other party in federal district court, setting forth its claims and the damages the band is seeking. In Wanton Success's case, there are certain tests created by courts that must be passed to prove the Copier copied its song, including substantial similarity of the works, and that the Copier had access to its work. (Usually a musicologist is hired as an expert witness to testify about the similar nature of the material.) Wanton Success must file within three years of Copier's release for a civil claim or five years for a criminal action.

As always in a case like this, it's best for the band to consult an attorney to ensure its rights are properly protected.

DEFENSES AVAILABLE IN INFRINGEMENT ACTIONS

The copying or sale of a copy of a copyrighted work is not always considered to be infringement. Congress has created exclusions to copyright, which will permit the use of a protected work in certain situations.

The Fair Use Defense

Perhaps the most prominent defense to copyright infringement is the *fair use* defense, which relates to certain uses of creative works that are deemed important to the advancement of society as a whole. Use for educational purposes, news reporting, research, and criticism are all examples of what may fall under the fair use doctrine. It is important to remember that fair use is only a *defense*, and there is no certain way to know in advance, without going to court, if a use will be deemed "fair." The Copyright Act sets forth a four-prong test for fair use:

1. The purpose and character of the use, including whether such use is of a commercial nature or is for nonprofit educational purposes;

2. The nature of the copyrighted work;

3. The amount and substantiality of the portion used in relation to the copyrighted work as a whole;

4. The effect of the use upon the potential market for or value of the copyrighted work.

—Copyright Act of 1976, 17 U.S.C. § 107

According to the U.S. Copyright Office, the 1961 "Report of the Register of Copyrights on the General Revision of the U.S. Copyright Law" cites examples of activities that courts have regarded as fair use, including:

...quotation of excerpts in a review or criticism for purposes of illustration or comment; quotation of short passages in a scholarly or technical work, for illustration or clarification of the author's observations; use in a parody of some of the content of the work parodied; summary of an address or article, with brief quotations, in a news report; reproduction by a library of a portion of a work to replace part of a damaged copy; reproduction by a teacher or student of a small part of a work to illustrate a lesson; reproduction of a work in legislative or judicial proceedings or reports; incidental and fortuitous reproduction, in a newsreel or broadcast, of a work located in the scene of an event being reported.

—www.copyright.gov

A SAMPLE ANALYSIS: *CAMPBELL AKA LUKE SKYYWALKER V. ACUFF-ROSE MUSIC, INC.*, SUPREME COURT OF THE UNITED STATES, 510 U.S. 569

In 1994, in a landmark case analysis of the fair use doctrine, the Supreme Court heard a case in which 2 Live Crew and their record label, Luke Skyywalker Records, were alleged to have infringed the rights of Acuff-Rose Publishing when they wrote and released a parody version of Roy Orbison's song "Pretty Woman." (Orbison and his co-writer had assigned their rights to Acuff-Rose Music, Inc. in 1964.)

In 1989, Luther Campbell, a member of 2 Live Crew, wrote a song called "Pretty Woman," he testified, "through comical lyrics, to satirize the original work." The band asked Acuff-Rose for permission to use the song, and offered to credit Acuff-Rose as the owner of the song, as well as to pay a fee for the use. Acuff-Rose refused to grant permission, and the band released the song anyway.

The next year, after nearly 250,000 copies of the song had been sold, Acuff-Rose sued 2 Live Crew and Luke Skyywalker Records, and the district court granted summary judgment (a judgment without a trial) for 2 Live Crew. The court viewed 2 Live Crew's song as a parody, and established that despite the band's commercial gain from the song, the band was protected by the fair use defense. The Court of Appeals for the Sixth Circuit reversed the decision, concluding that the song's "blatantly commercial purpose prevents this parody from being a fair use."

The Supreme Court, in its analysis, offered a historical perspective on the purpose of the fair use doctrine:

> From the infancy of copyright protection, some opportunity for fair use of copyrighted materials has been thought necessary to fulfill copyright's very purpose, "to promote the Progress of Science and useful Arts…." U.S. Const., Art I, § 8, cl.8. For as Justice Story explained, "in truth, in literature, in science and in art, there are, and can be, few, if any, things, which in an abstract sense, are strictly new and original throughout. Every book in literature, science and art, borrows, and must necessarily borrow, and use much which was well known and used before."
>
> —*Emerson v. Davies*, 8 F. Cas 615, 619 (No.4, 436)
> (C.C.D. Mass 1845)

> *... Congress meant § 107 to restate the present judicial
> doctrine of fair use, not to change, narrow, or enlarge it in
> any way and intended that courts continue the common law
> tradition of fair use adjudication. The fair use doctrine thus
> "permits [and requires] courts to avoid rigid application of the
> copyright statute when, on occasion, it would stifle the very
> creativity which that law is designed to foster."*
> —*Stewart v. Abend*, 495 U.S. 207, 236 (1990) [14]

The court went on to analyze 2 Live Crew's version of the song through the four-prong test for fair use. Under the first test, the court noted that "transformative" works may lessen the significance of other factors such as commercialism. The court found that parodies, as "transformative" works, can provide social benefit, and are entitled to present a legitimate fair use defense. Their opinion noted that merely because a work was used for commercial purposes did not necessarily preclude a fair use defense, given that news reporting, research, teaching, and education are "generally conducted for a profit" in this country.

The second factor, according to the court, was satisfied. Parodies by their nature copy "publicly known, expressive works."

When analyzing the third factor, "the amount and substantiality of the portion used in relation to the copyrighted work as a whole," the court found that a parody must sometimes use the "heart" of a work in order to conjure up the original in order for listeners to correctly make the object of the parody recognizable. Despite the fact that 2 Live Crew copied the signature bass riff of the original "Pretty Woman," they had added "distinctive sounds," interposing "scraper" noise, overlaying the music with solos in different keys, and altering the drum beat. It found that the parody itself had added enough substantial elements, when compared to the original, to offset the fact that 2 Live Crew had taken the "heart" of the song.

Finally, the court drew a correlation to a "scathing theater review" when scrutinizing the song under the fourth lens of the test, "the effect of the use upon the potential market for or value of the copyrighted work" and noted that a court must distinguish between "biting criticism [that merely] suppresses demand and copyright infringement which usurps it." In other words, a parody typically

---

14 *Campbell AKA Luke Skyywalker v. Acuff-Rose Music, Inc.*, Supreme Court of the United States, 510 U.S. 569]

does not serve as a substitute for the original, but instead creates its own market. The court also addressed whether or not a parody might have affected the market for a rap derivative work of "Pretty Woman," but that neither side had introduced evidence on this aspect in the trial.

Ultimately, the court decided that 2 Live Crew's version of "Pretty Woman" could be a fair one, and sent the case back to the Court of Appeals for a holding consistent with the Supreme Court's analysis. The parties later settled out of court. The case was pivotal because it upheld the right to create parodies without fear of infringement suits (assuming such parodies manage to pass the four-part test set forth in Section 107 of the Copyright Act).

(The court, in a rare show of humor, explicitly stated that they would not evaluate the quality of a parody, and that "whether, going beyond that, parody is in good taste or bad does not and should not matter to fair use.")

Original:
Pretty woman, walking down the street,
Pretty Woman, the kind I like to meet,
Pretty Woman, I don't believe you,
You're not the truth,
No one could look as good as you Mercy

2 Live Crew:
Pretty woman, walkin' down the street,
Pretty woman, girl you look so sweet,
Pretty woman, you bring me down to that knee,
Pretty woman, you make me wanna beg please,
Oh pretty woman

In recorded music, the fair use defense is commonly used to defend parodies (think Al Yankovic) and the use of certain portions. There is, however, a fine line between fair use and the need for a sampling license. We'll discuss sampling (the use of one song within another) in chapter 3.

Copyright also provides a defense for those who wish to sell their individual copy of a particular work. Under the *first sale* doctrine, a creator should only profit from the first sale of his or her original work (or a particular copy). The Copyright Act states:

> ...the owner of a particular copy or phonorecord lawfully made under this title, or any person authorized by such owner, is entitled, without the authority of the copyright owner, to sell or otherwise dispose of the possession of that copy or phonorecord.

—Copyright Act of 1976, 17 U.S.C. § 109(a)

This means that despite the efforts of artists such as Garth Brooks, who decried CD resale shops in the late 1990s for reducing revenue streams to artists and songwriters, owners of a particular copy may sell their copy of a particular work to whomever they choose, without penalty.

The first sale doctrine has also faced some recent challenges in the online space from companies like ReDigi, which believed the first sale doctrine should also apply to digital files. ReDigi's service allowed users to sell their copy of an MP3 or other digital content file. In 2013, Capitol Records won a case against the company, with the court stating that it is impossible to transfer a copy of a digital file without making a copy, which then violates the first sale doctrine. ReDigi appealed to the Second Circuit Court of Appeals, where the company lost again in 2018, and the Supreme Court in 2019 declined to hear a further appeal, leaving the lower court's ruling to stand. However, in Europe in a similar case in 2012, *UsedSoft GmbH v. Oracle International Corp.*, the European Court of Justice allowed the digital resale of software. The cases are good examples of the complexities of mixing copyright with new technologies, which we will discuss further in chapter 11.

SELLING USED STUFF

Question: If copyright protects a creator's ability to manufacture and distribute copies of his or her work, why can I sell my used Rolling Stone CDs or my Van Gogh print?

Answer: *The first sale doctrine allows owners of a particular copy of a work to sell that particular copy of the work. In essence, a copyright holder is by law only entitled to profit from the first sale of each individual copy of his or her work.*

INTERNATIONAL PROTECTION OF COPYRIGHT

American creators and copyright owners may wonder if their works are protected overseas and in foreign countries, since the United States Congress passed the copyright law originally covering their work. To solve this issue, a number of international treaties have been signed to ensure copyright protection of works in other jurisdictions. Despite the treaties, while there are certainly some themes that cross borders (the fundamental copyright law basics, for example), applicable law and business practices vary widely from territory to territory. The way music is licensed for public performance, and the right of sound recording copyright holders to receive royalties for radio play, for example, is significantly different overseas. (We'll discuss some of these differences in chapter 6.)

Copyright provides exclusive rights to authors (or their assignees) and protects creative works. But how can copyright work successfully on a global scale in our "Digital Age" when each country has its own laws? What are the various stakeholders in the music distribution chain to do in an effort to properly manage these multiple variables? While we will try to cover the basics in this book, if you plan to cross borders, you are best advised to seek professional consultation along the way. Requirements from country to country—as well as ownership rights—may vary greatly. With infringement and investment stakes as high as they are, it is wise to be as informed as possible when working in unfamiliar territories.

Berne Convention

Perhaps the most important international copyright treaty is the Berne Convention, which resulted from an international agreement first accepted in 1886 at Berne, Switzerland. In short, the treaty provides that an author of a work is entitled to the same protections as a domestic author in any country that is a signatory to the Convention. The treaty has 167 members, but despite its widespread acceptance, the United States did not become an official party to the Berne Convention until 103 years later, in 1989. Under Berne, although the copyright law of the country will apply whenever a claim is applied, *in no event will the duration of copyright protection extend beyond whatever it would be in the country of origin of the work* (known as the "rule of the shorter term").

Geneva Convention

Equally important to our discussion of international copyright and music is the Geneva Convention, which specifically requires each signatory to protect authors of "phonograms" (i.e., sound recordings) against the making, importation, or distribution of duplicates of their works without permission. The United States became a member of the Geneva Convention in 1974.

Rome Convention

The 1963 Rome Convention established certain protections that were meant to extend beyond those created by the Berne Convention in response to new technologies. In general, performers (actors, singers, musicians, dancers, and other people who perform literary or artistic works), producers, and broadcasters are protected against the broadcasting and the communication to the public of their live performance, the fixation of their live performance, and the reproduction of such a fixation if they have not explicitly consented. The United States is not yet a signatory to the Rome Convention, and is not compliant in part because sound recordings do not have a public performance right on terrestrial radio in the U.S.

Smaller Treaties

Finally, other smaller treaties such as the Buenos Aires Convention also exist. The Buenos Aires Convention provides for mutual recognition of copyrights in countries in Latin America and the United States. At this time, however, all parties to the Buenos Aires Convention are also parties to the Berne Convention.

CHAPTER 3

Copyright in Music

As we saw in chapter 2, today, the recorded music industry is built on two major copyrights:

1. the copyright in the musical work (i.e., the song: music and lyrics)

2. the copyright in the sound recording (i.e., the recorded performance, or an artist's interpretation of the song)

Each of these provides the copyright owner of a musical composition or a sound recording with the same exclusive rights granted to all copyright holders under copyright law, with two exceptions: (a) there is no right of public display for a sound recording, due to the very nature of the work; and (b) there is no right of public performance for sound recordings other than in digital transmissions. This distinction between the two copyrights is important, because the rights granted to musical works are more encompassing than those of sound recordings.

There is also a differentiation in the way we analyze how copyright owners and administrators (such as record labels and music publishers) monetize their copyright, because different rules apply to each copyright. For example, owners of music publishing copyrights receive a payment for public performances on traditional "over-the-air" radio and television broadcasts, while sound recording copyright holders do not. Incidentally, nearly every country around the world except the United States requires public performance royalties to be paid to sound recording copyright holders for all broadcasts. Several bills have been introduced in Congress to change this and provide a performance right for sound recordings, but the terrestrial radio lobby has been successful in blocking these attempts. In 2012 and 2013, Clear Channel (America's largest radio conglomerate, with over 1,200 radio stations) struck agreements with some major and independent record labels, including Warner Music Group and Big Machine, to pay a performance right for sound recordings owned by these labels as part of broader deals encompassing both terrestrial and online performances on Clear Channel's stations, many of which broadcast over the Internet. The deals help to cap and make predictable the payments for online radio listens, which, absent such deals, are regulated by the Copyright Royalty Board to be a per play/per listener fee.

MUSICAL WORKS

The exclusive right of public performance for musical works is one of the six rights of a copyright holder, as we saw in chapter 2. Publishing companies, or songwriters, or whoever the copyright holders may be, are entitled to a fee every time their musical work is performed publicly. Examples of public performance range from radio play to live performances to online streaming.

Congress, however, did not initially include a mechanism for musical works rights holders to be paid for public performances. Think of the logistics: thousands of broadcasters, concert halls, restaurants, and other live venues negotiating separately for each song they publicly perform. PROs solve this problem, but PROs became widely used as a result of litigation. In a 1922 case against Bamberger's Department Store in Newark, New Jersey, courts held that the store was broadcasting music throughout its store from a radio station, WOR, and that it was doing so for commercial gain. The performance of the copyrighted song on the radio was therefore a public performance, meaning copyright owners could demand payment for one of their exclusive rights: public performance. The ruling led to the rapid growth of ASCAP, which had been founded in 1914 by songwriters and publishers, as venues needed a method to clear public performance licenses without going to each publisher. ASCAP today is one of three main PROs in the United States collecting public performance royalties for writers from radio, television, film, and live-venue performances. As mentioned earlier, each PRO uses a complicated formula, mostly based on airplay, to determine how much each writer should be paid every accounting period.

The other two large American PROs in existence today, BMI and SESAC, also developed in the twentieth century. SESAC was formed in 1930 to license European works in the United States. BMI was formed by radio broadcasters as an alternative to ASCAP in 1939, and continues to be owned and operated by major broadcasters today, although it operates as a non-profit. Conversely to ASCAP and BMI, SESAC is the only "for-profit" collecting society. Based in Nashville and owned by private investors, SESAC maintains a strategy of obtaining rights to popular music and using them as leverage in negotiations with broadcasters.

BMI and ASCAP both operate under "consent decrees" from the U.S. government. After complaints of antitrust behavior under the Sherman Act, the two companies entered into these consent decrees in 1941, which allowed them to operate but required certain restrictions:

1. They cannot obtain from songwriters and publishers of music the exclusive right to license public performances of their works, meaning the rights holders can "go direct."

2. They cannot seek payments for programs that do not contain their music.

3. They cannot discriminate between users who are "similarly situated."

4. They must distribute royalties to members in a "fair and non-discriminatory manner."

The consent decrees today allow for any party seeking a license from ASCAP or BMI who cannot come to terms to seek a ruling from a court, which will set the rate. In 2020, the Justice Department finished a review of the ASCAP and BMI consent decrees and chose to keep them in place.

Finally, two newcomers to the market, Global Music Rights and Kobalt Music Group's newly positioned AMRA, focus their collection of public performance royalties for musical works owners on the digital market. GMR claims their smaller size allows for better representation and payoffs for their members, while AMRA is focused on increasing revenue streams through better transparency in payouts.

Note that, unlike the competitive atmosphere in the United States, in most countries around the world, a single performing society exists to collect and distribute public performance royalties.

SHOULD I JOIN A PRO?

Question: We are a small independent band, and we write our own material. Our manager advised us to register with a PRO to make more money. What does this mean? Will we actually make money by doing this? Does it cost anything?

Answer: *If you are a writer or owner of the copyright in a song or other musical composition, you should consider joining a PRO if your work might be performed publicly in a broadcast medium such as radio or television, played live at music venues, or streamed online. PROs, which are free to join, generally handle blanket clearance services for the public performance of compositions. Venues (bars, restaurants, retail stores) and services (online services including ad supported and subscription on-demand streaming services) "publicly perform" compositions when they play music for customers. PROs collect negotiated royalty fees from venues and services and distribute them to the appropriate rights holders.*

Your manager is suggesting that you register with a PRO so that you can collect royalties for public performance of your compositions. Again, PROs are free to join. The admission/registration process with any of them is easy and reasonable and should, if managed properly, result in an additional revenue stream for writers. ASCAP, for example, processes hundreds of millions of dollars in royalties for its members annually.

There are differences in each PRO in the U.S. ASCAP and BMI are not-for-profit, while SESAC is a for-profit entity that requires an invitation to join. ASCAP was formed by music creators in 1914, and is 100 percent member-owned, while BMI was founded as a competitor to ASCAP in 1939 by radio executives who wanted to provide rights holders an alternative to ASCAP.

- *Today, ASCAP and BMI are open to all writers. Prospective members need only download a membership from their respective websites.*
- *Membership in SESAC and Global Music Rights is by invitation only. AMRA's availability is unknown as of this writing.*
- *ASCAP and BMI administer the vast majority of compositions commercially available in the United States.*
- *Each company uses a different formula to compute royalty payments to writers. Writers may only belong to one society at a time.*

For more information on each, visit their websites at www.ascap.com, www.bmi.com, www.sesac.com, www.amra-music.com, and www.global musicrights.com.

Of additional importance to writers is the ability to license their work for inclusion on a sound recording. This license to reproduce a musical composition is called a *mechanical license*, and copyright holders may negotiate whatever rate they desire with the record label or distributor of sound recordings. However, Congress has provided for what is called a "compulsory mechanical license" for musical works. This means that anyone can make and release his or her own sound recording of a musical work once that work has already been distributed to the public, as long as mechanical royalties are paid at the minimum rate or as negotiated with the musical composition copyright holder. (The minimum rate in the U.S. as of 2021 is 9.1 cents per song per album manufactured or track sold, or 1.75 cents per minute for tracks in excess of five minutes long. Overseas, the mechanical rate is typically a percentage of revenue. This methodology has now been adopted by the U.S. for mechanical royalties from streaming services, which we will discuss a bit later.)

> When phonorecords of a nondramatic musical work have been distributed to the public in the United States under the authority of the copyright owner, any other person, including those who make phonorecords or digital phonorecord deliveries, may, by complying with the provisions of this section, obtain a compulsory license only if his or her primary purpose in making phonorecords is to distribute them to the public for private use, including by means of digital phonorecord delivery.

—Copyright Act of 1976, 17 U.S.C. § 115(a)(1)

Congress has specifically included "digital phonorecord deliveries" in the compulsory licensing scheme, which means that writers are paid at the same mechanical royalty rate for sales on iTunes or other online download services as they would be for the sale of a compact disc. The Harry Fox Agency (HFA) currently serves as a clearinghouse for mechanical licenses in the United States, representing over 37,000 publishers and offering licensees the ability to procure mechanical licenses from a single source rather than contacting each music publisher individually.

A *compulsory license* will allow an artist to record a song in their own style, as long as fundamental changes to the song, such as significant lyrical changes, are not made. Also, note that the re-recording of a musical work in a style slightly different than that of the original will not confer the rights of a derivative work onto the new work. This allows artists who "cover" a song to alter its style (within the confines of the law) without running up against the exclusive right of the copyright owner to prepare derivative works. It also means that the cover artist will not have any rights in their version of the musical work, even though they may have altered its style slightly.

```
A compulsory license includes the privilege of
making a musical arrangement of the work to the
extent necessary to conform it to the style or
manner of interpretation of the performance
involved, but the arrangement shall not change
the basic melody or fundamental character of the
work, and shall not be subject to protection as
a derivative work under this title, except with
the express consent of the copyright owner.
```

—Copyright Act of 1976, 17 U.S.C. § 115(a)(2)

COVERING SONGS IN A DIFFERENT STYLE

Question: Wanton Success wants to cover Snoop Dogg's "Gin and Juice" as a folk song. Is the band able to record the song in such a different light without permission from Snoop Dogg or the other writers?

Answer: *Yes, as long as the basic melody and character of the work are not changed, and mechanical license payments are made to Snoop Dogg (or the current owner of the copyright in the "Gin and Juice" composition).*

Record labels will frequently ask artists who are also writers of their own material for a "controlled composition" clause in their recording agreement. Labels claim that since they are helping the writer/artist distribute the songs they've written and earn mechanical royalties, the label should receive mechanical licenses for the songs controlled by the artist (thus the term "controlled compositions") at a reduced rate. This rate is usually 75 percent of the statutory mechanical rate.

Similarly, record labels will frequently impose a cap on the number of compositions that may be "payable" per album (usually ten songs for a single-disc album), fix the payable rate at the established rate at the time of release (sometimes even fixed at time of delivery of masters—meaning that the artist won't get the benefit of any increases to the statutory rate), and even limit the number of royalty bearing minutes per recording. These methods are employed in negotiations at a time of great leverage to ensure that the labels' songwriter royalty costs are managed and mitigated.

It is important to note that many of these restrictions may not apply to digital-only streams. Also keep in mind that because there is a temporary reproduction in a stream, mechanical licenses *are* required for streaming.

Record labels typically do not directly grant the license for the composition, a right that can only be granted by the music publisher or other holder of that composition right. Except for online streaming, record labels typically collect this separate fee, however, with an assurance (typically in the form of a representation or warranty) that they will pass the fee for the composition through to the composition right holder. Current mechanical rates are:

TYPE OF MECHANICAL LICENSE	UNITED STATES COMPULSORY LICENSE RATE
Songs downloaded or sold in physical format (less than 5 minutes)	9.1 cents
Songs downloaded or sold in physical format (more than 5 minutes)	1.75 cents per minute
Limited downloads	Formula under 37 C.F.R. §385.21
Interactive streaming	Formula under 37 C.F.R. §385.21

FIG. 3.1. Rates for Different Mechanical Licenses

MUSIC MODERNIZATION ACT

In 2018, Congress passed the most substantive change to copyright law in the United States pertaining to music since the passage of the Copyright Act of 1976, the Music Modernization Act (MMA). The law substantially changed the compulsory mechanical licensing structure for streaming music.

The prior structure was imperfect due to a lack of readily available rights information. Due to the Berne Convention, which requires that copyright laws in its member countries cannot require registration as a prerequisite for protection, and traditional industry practices that have led to the protection of ownership information as proprietary information, existing copyright databases were difficult to access, and often inaccurate and/or incomplete. This made the licensing process difficult for DSPs with millions of works available on their platforms.

Many rights owners claimed to have never received mechanical royalty payments as required under the law, despite availability of their works on DSPs. Large class-action lawsuits by songwriters and publishers were filed in the U.S. (and later settled for tens of millions of dollars) against Spotify, which was accused of not properly licensing musical works and therefore infringing the rights of owners whose musical works were available on the platform. This discrepancy largely came about due to the distribution of sound recordings by record labels without the appropriate or correct underlying musical work metadata.

The MMA created a non-profit Music Licensing Collective (MLC), which launched in 2021 and is responsible for issuing blanket licenses to DSPs and collecting and disbursing compulsory mechanical royalties for music publishing to the correct owners. Blanket licenses are available for all uses for which compulsory mechanical licensing is available in the U.S. Provided they enter into the blanket license, DSPs no longer have liability for the use of such works or face the risk of infringement claims and possibility of large class-action lawsuits for failure to pay mechanical royalties.

The MLC's blanket licenses cover all musical works available for compulsory license unless those works are covered by a voluntary license. Copyright owners (whether U.S.-based or foreign, non-published or published works) must register with the MLC in order to receive their U.S. mechanical royalty payments. However, owners of musical works may use another entity to administer voluntary licenses and choose not to use the MLC's blanket license system.

USING THE MLC

Question: What is the Mechanical Licensing Collective? How do I use it to get paid for my songs that are available on Spotify/Apple/Deezer/TIDAL?

Answer: *The Mechanical Licensing Collective (MLC) was mandated by the Music Modernization Act of 2018. It allows any songwriter, U.S. or foreign, to register and collect their mechanical royalties. To collect your royalties, visit the MLC website at themlc.com and register your works. Various identifying information may be needed; due to the developing nature of the platform, requirements change from time to time. This will enable you to receive your share of songwriting (mechanical) royalties held by DSPs on your behalf. Don't forget to also register to collect your performance royalties through a PRO (ASCAP/BMI/SESAC/GMR, etc.), and don't delay in registering, as unclaimed royalties are eventually paid out to other copyright owners if the proper owners cannot be identified in the MLC system.*

The MMA also changed some of the rate-setting considerations for the Copyright Royalty Board (CRB) (discussed on the following pages), repeals Section 114(f), and now requires the CRB to consider a willing buyer/willing seller standard and rates for sound recordings when setting royalty rates. This empowers musical composition copyright holders who have traditionally been less able to set free market rates in the past.

ROYALTIES FOR COVERED SONGS

Question: A songwriter composed an entire album of compositions for the popular sixties band, the Bent. For the next three decades, the songwriter, who maintains copyright ownership, collected dwindling mechanical royalties on a per-song basis from the record label that distributed the album. In 2013, three songs from the original album by the Bent were re-recorded as covers by a pop artist whose album is distributed by a different label. The sales and streams of these cover recordings have been significant. Is the songwriter entitled to mechanical royalties for sales and streams of the covers? Who should the songwriter contact to collect such royalties?

Answer: *Yes, the songwriter is absolutely entitled to mechanical royalties in the amount of 9.1 cents per track on download sales. (The songwriter should contact the record label distributing the pop artist's album to collect such fees on both a retroactive and going-forward basis. The songwriter should also consider contacting DSPs and the MLC about mechanical royalty payments on streams.)*

In the Copyright Act, Congress provided for a mechanism to appoint "Copyright Royalty Judges" who are responsible for setting and adjusting royalty rates, such as the compulsory mechanical license, as provided for in sections 114, 115, 116, 118, and 119 of the Copyright Act. The Librarian of Congress appoints the three judges, who serve full-time, and generally the judges are required to calculate the rates to achieve certain objectives:

(A) To maximize the availability of creative works to the public;

(B) To afford the copyright owner a fair return for his or her creative work and the copyright user a fair income under existing economic conditions;

(C) To reflect the relative roles of the copyright owner and the copyright user in the product made available to the public with respect to relative creative contribution, technological contribution, capital investment, cost, risk, and contribution to the opening of new markets for creative expression and media for their communication;

(D) To minimize any disruptive impact on the structure of the industries involved and on generally prevailing industry practices.

—Copyright Act of 1976, 17 U.S.C. § 801(b)(1)

SOUND RECORDINGS

While protections under the Copyright Act have served rights holders well for decades, new technologies, unanticipated at the time the Act was written, have raised questions of how to appropriately protect rights in the digital age, and new legislation is regularly considered to address these concerns. For example, as mentioned earlier, the development of the DAT led to the Audio Home Recording Act of 1992, which placed levies on manufacturers whose products might promote infringement. The DAT was widely cited as the first technology to allow repeated copying without loss of quality, and for that reason, labels and musicians lobbied Congress for an amendment to the Copyright Act.

The "Audio Home Recording Act" provides for a 2 percent royalty on digital audio recording devices. Devices, however, are so narrowly defined in the bill that it means, literally, only DAT players. Further, the law requires manufacturers of blank media (such as blank CDs) to pay a 3 percent royalty on sales. The Copyright Office collects the money and pays it out to musical composition and sound recording copyright holders, as well as to non-featured musicians who are members of the American Federation of Musicians (AFM) or American Federation of Television and Radio Artists (AFTRA) unions, who receive a small share.

The law also required manufacturers of DAT players to include a serial copy management system, preventing the recording of subsequent-generation tapes from the original DAT copy. There is no restriction on copying in analog formats.

> The royalty payment due under section 1003 for each digital audio recording device imported into and distributed in the United States, or manufactured and distributed in the United States, shall be 2 percent of the transfer price. Only the first person to manufacture and distribute or import and distribute such device shall be required to pay the royalty with respect to such device.
>
> *—Copyright Act of 1976, 17 U.S.C. § 1004(a)(1)*

> The royalty payments deposited pursuant to section 1005 shall, in accordance with the procedures specified in section 1007, be distributed to any interested copyright party—(1) whose musical work or sound recording has been—(A) embodied in a digital musical recording or an analog musical recording lawfully made under this title that has been distributed, and (B) distributed in the form of digital musical recordings or analog musical recordings or disseminated to the public in transmissions, during the period to which such payments pertain; and (2) who has filed a claim under Section 1007.
>
> *—Copyright Act of 1976, 17 U.S.C. § 1006(a)*

FEES FROM HARDWARE MANUFACTURERS?

We have seen efforts by labels, outside copyright law, to receive royalties on the sale of devices (the practice is already commonplace for patents, as well as for the use of communication protocols and encoding formats like MP3). Some labels in 2006 reportedly requested a royalty from Microsoft on the sales of the company's Zune portable music player as part of a licensing arrangement for their catalogue of music. This was the first known attempt to tax new hardware since the Audio Home Recording Act of 1992 was passed, and they were reportedly successful in their negotiations.

While Congress responded to DAT technologies with a specific solution, other problems are not always easily resolved. Amendments and new legislation are regularly introduced each year to Congress, with very few surviving past the initial Congres-sional committee review, and even fewer becoming law. We'll discuss some of these attempts to update the law later in the book.

More changes affecting sound recordings did ensue when digital transmissions of music became available online in the mid 1990s. Congress passed the DPRSRA, an amendment to the Copyright Act, in 1995, which for the first time established a public performance royalty right for the holders of sound recording copyrights. This means that most publicly available digital transmissions of a sound recording, such as Internet radio and satellite radio, now require a performance royalty payment to the recording's owner. Interactive and subscription services such as satellite radio, digital cable (except retransmission of broadcast television), and on-demand online music are all subject to the provision.

The amendment also provided for a collective licensing organ-ization for sound recording performance royalties, so that indivi-dual licensing would not be necessary. SoundExchange is a not-for-profit collective licensing organization designated by the Librarian of Congress to have exclusive authority to collect the royalties due for non-interactive digital transmissions of sound recordings (in other words, a PRO for these transmissions). If you are a sound recording copyright holder, and your music is performed digitally via DMCA compliant Internet radio (see chapter 10), you are entitled to receive royalty payments from SoundExchange; see the appendix for registration and contact information for

SoundExchange. On-demand online streaming is also subject to the performance right, but licenses are negotiated with each copyright holder and royalties do not flow through SoundExchange.

Part of the impetus for the DPRSRA was a fear by record labels of substitution—that consumers could get the recordings or music in a different fashion and would no longer be buying recorded music (much like the labels' concerns about radio in the 1920s). The interactive services are, however, unlike radio, and are actually substitutive for the purchase of recordings, given their on-demand nature. As Robert Gorman and Jane Ginsburg note in their treatise on copyright:

> *What precipitated the amendment was the introduction of technology allowing for digital audio transmissions to home subscribers (fully akin to cable-television subscribers) who receive the sounds of top quality digital sound recordings and who may well thus forego the purchase of cassettes and compact discs. In part it was assumed that many digital-audio subscribers would indulge in home taping. It was understood by the congressional proponents of the legislation that "interactive" audio services would allow subscribers to call up any desired digital recordings at any time (i.e., pay-per-listen or audio-on-demand, the equivalent of pay-per-view for cable subscribers) and thus altogether displace the need to purchase recordings.*[1]

Despite complaints by Americans about Congress, they are to be given credit for foreseeing the future of music distribution and consumption in the very early days of the Internet, and passing the DPRSRA in 1995 before there was a lobbying group against it. Imagine the outcry from Pandora and Spotify if Congress was trying to make that change today!

---

1   Gorman, Robert and Ginsburg, Jane C. *Copyright: Cases and Materials.* Fifth Edition. Charlottesville: Lexis Law Publishing, 1999.

ROYALTIES ON WEBCASTS

Rates for webcasting have been a contentious issue since the passage of the DPRSRA. In 2007, the Copyright Royalty Board (CRB) substantially increased fees for DMCA-compliant radio, leading to the Webcaster Settlement Act, which established several different categories of broadcasters (including "small webcasters") and set rates at a different level for each. The settlement covered fees to be paid from 2006 to 2015. In June 2021, the CRB set new rates valid through 2025. The decision makes no mention of small webcasters and sets a broadly applicable per stream rate of $.0021 for non-subscription streaming and $.0026 for subscription streams. The decision includes a provision for small, non-profit webcasters, and for the first time, rates will be indexed for inflation.

The MMA granted royalty rights to pre-1972 sound recordings, which in the past had not been covered by the public performance right in sound recordings because these works did not have federal copyright protection, due to an anomaly in the law. (Federal copyright protection for these works did not begin until 1972.) These sound recordings are now eligible for streaming public performance royalties; until the change in the law, there had been a number of lawsuits claiming these royalties under state law. Perhaps the most publicized were cases by the Turtles against SiriusXM filed in both Florida and California.

Another distinction between musical works and sound recordings lies in section 114 of the Copyright Act, which sets forth limitations on rights in sound recordings. One provision makes it explicitly clear that an owner of a sound recording has no authority to prevent others from creating a sound recording with similar sounds. This means that no record label can prevent another from recording a cover of a song, as long as the owner of the copyright in the musical work properly authorizes such a recording. In other words, a cover song cannot be a derivative work of the original sound recording.

The exclusive rights of the owner of copyright in a sound recording under clauses (1) and (2) of section 106 do not extend to the making or dupli-cation of another sound recording that consists entirely of an independent fixation of other

sounds, even though such sounds imitate or simu-
late those in the copyrighted sound recording.

*—Copyright Act of 1976, 17 U.S.C. § 114(b) "Use of Music in
Television, Video Games, and Film"*

TRADITIONAL MODEL FOR TELEVISION, FILM, AND VIDEO GAME LICENSING

As the music industry has changed, so have outlets for the release and delivery of music to listeners. One shift has been the recent dramatic increase in the amount of music used in television, film, and video games.

Despite the differences in the two types of music copyrights, the use of music in film and television is rather simple. Both the copyright for sound recordings and musical works are entitled to payment streams, with a few differences.

Two rights are needed to include the musical compositions in an audiovisual work: (a) the right to synchronize the music with the video (commonly called the "sync license"), and (b) a license to publicly perform the music. The synchronization license is granted by the publisher or copyright owner, and gives the licensee the right to attach the music to the video (or synchronize it). It's usually a flat fee paid to the musical composition copyright owner.

The broadcast, or public performance of the musical compo-sition in the audiovisual work, will trigger royalty payments to the applicable PRO, resulting in the second stream of revenue.

Separately, sound recordings are licensed from the owner via a master use license, which grants the video owner the right to use the master recording in the audiovisual work. Public performance royalties may also be applicable if the broadcast is a digital transmission, under the DPRSRA. Finally, don't forget that DVDs, video games, and sales of videos through digital downloads all require a mechanical license for the reproduction of the musical composition.

SHOULD I LET MY RECORD LABEL DO MY SYNCHRONIZATION LICENSE DEALS?

Question: A record label that has been courting our band since our tour last summer finally sent me a letter agreement pursuant to which they want me to agree to give them all synchronization license rights for my musical works in exchange for a 25 percent share that would come to me. Should I sign it?

Answer: *It depends. As with all record label deal negotiations, what you decide to do here depends on what party has the leverage in the negotiations. If you are well positioned, this is something on which you should push back. Record labels rarely, if ever, play a role in finding or negotiating what can be profitable synchronization deals; this is something typically done by a music publisher appointed to the task by the original author (or artist) or by the artist themselves. It is, in my general opinion, unreasonable for a record label to take any of these royalties, and certainly not 75 percent. I recommend that you push back on this term and try to keep this royalty pool to yourself. At minimum, you should keep the majority of revenue and let the label have 25 percent, provided that they play some role in finding and/or negotiating for this license.*

In practice, using Guitar Hero as an example, Harmonix (the manufacturer of the popular Guitar Hero, Dance Central, and Rock Band video games) must procure mechanical licenses and pay royalties to the owner of the musical composition copyright for the sales of each game that contains the composition. They'll also need a synchronization license to synchronize the composition to the visual images in the game, and a master use license for any portions of the sound recording they may use. This is all in addition to the rights to use the artist's name, and in some cases, their image.

SAMPLING, MASH-UPS, AND EDITABLE TRACKS: DO YOU NEED A LICENSE?

Sampling another's music on your own record also requires licenses for the use of the master recording and musical composition. The musical composition copyright holder and the sound recording copyright owner will require a payment of royalties, but this amount is often based on the extent of the use in the new material. Licenses for samples are typically negotiated on a case-by-case basis and, in the case of musical compositions, usually results in the owner of the sampled composition being given a negotiated percentage of the newly created work. There is no amount of work that can be used for free. In the EU, the Court of Justice of the European Union ruled in a case involving Kraftwerk in 2019 that no sample can be used without permission unless it is modified to be unrecognizable.

IS A SAMPLE INFRINGING?

Question: Somebody told me that if our band uses less than five seconds of another song as a sample, we don't need to get that cleared. Is that true? What can happen if we don't get it cleared?

Answer: *No, this is not true. There is no minimum duration, or minimum number of bars or notes, that triggers a need for a license. As has been shown in litigation, even a couple of notes can be considered a sample that requires a license to be legally used. However, use of a song may be considered fair use, depending on the context of the use.*

Some artists have offered multitrack downloads of songs, which allow fans to create their own remixes of the material. (Trent Reznor made news a few years ago when his band Nine Inch Nails released a number of multitrack files to his fans for free.) Other downloadable and online programs allow users to mix two songs together, creating a combination of the two (or more) songs. With the sound recording copyright owner's permission, this is perfectly legal. Software programs that sell beats or stems also usually include a full license for users to create new works using their products.

However, when songs and individual instrument tracks are remixed without copyright permission, a question of legality arises. The new material is clearly a derivative work of the original song(s), but is it a fair use? Is it transformative? What is the impact of the new song on the market for original material? Overseas, a moral rights issue may also arise if the work is "changed" (in countries that offer moral rights protection for creators; the U.S. does not).

One American artist, Girl Talk, has made a career of creating full songs that consist completely of small snippets of other songs.

Selling tens of thousands of albums, and often performing in front of thousands of fans, his art has yet to be challenged legally by copyright owners. Some surmise that this is due to a fear they'll lose based on a fair use defense, setting a legal precedent that could open floodgates. Stay tuned, as this is sure to be an interesting topic in years to come.

CHAPTER 4

What Is a "Copy" and
What Is a "Performance"?

As mentioned earlier, two of the exclusive rights provided to a copyright holder are the rights to:

- copy or control the copying of his or her work and
- control the distribution of copies of a work.

WHAT IS A "COPY"?

In a world of digital distribution and computer files, how do you define a "copy" when the copy is in soft copy, rather than hard copy? This question is one of the largest challenges posed today by digital distribution. For example, as we saw, the first sale doctrine would seem to indicate that a person can sell his or her "copy" of a sound recording, but how would this apply online? It's theoretically impossible, today, to transfer a file to another without making a new copy of it before deleting the original. Therefore, the first sale doctrine becomes impossible to apply to soft copies transmitted to another person, because it's not the original file.

CAN YOU RESELL MUSIC FILES?

Question: Joe Smith buys a copy of Adele's "Hello" from the iTunes music store. Joe later decides he wants to sell his soft copy of the song to Janet Williams. Can he do this?

Answer: *Theoretically, under the first sale doctrine, Joe can sell his copy, but he'll have to delete his copy. However, it would be impossible for Joe to actually give his file to Janet without also giving her his device on which the song was loaded, because a copy would be necessary. Even if Joe deletes the song from his computer as soon as he's sent the file to Janet, he has still infringed the right of the copyright holder to restrict copying of the work.*

Copying is also an issue for companies who provide digital delivery services. The concept of a "server copy," or copies created internally by music services to facilitate their delivery of music (oftentimes, copies will be needed on multiple computer servers) has been the subject of much discussion as technology develops. Some cases have held that a license is necessary to make a server copy, although the reality is that most rights owners ignore this technicality as long as the digital server has performance and mechanical licenses.

In contradiction, the Copyright Act does, however, explicitly stipulate that it is not infringement for broadcast, over-the-air services to create limited copies of copyrighted works as necessary for the purpose of facilitating their services, if the other required licenses are in place:

- Notwithstanding the provisions of section 106, and except in the case of a motion picture or other audiovisual work, it is not an infringement of copyright for a transmitting organization entitled to transmit to the public a performance or display of a work, under a license, including a statutory license under section 114(f), or transfer of the copyright or under the limitations on exclusive rights in sound recordings specified by section 114(a) or for a transmitting organization that is a broadcast radio or television station licensed as such by the Federal Communications Commission and that makes a broadcast transmission of a performance of a sound recording in a digital format on a non-subscription basis, to make no more than one copy or phonorecord of a particular transmission program embodying the performance or display, if: the copy or phonorecord is retained and used solely by the transmitting organization that made it, and no further copies or phonorecords are reproduced from it; and

- The copy or phonorecord is used solely for the transmitting organization's own transmissions within its local service area, or for purposes of archival preservation or security; and

- Unless preserved exclusively for archival purposes, the copy or phonorecord is destroyed within six months from the date the transmission program was first transmitted to the public.

—Copyright Act of 1976, 17 U.S.C. § 112(a)

Further, in section 112(e) of the Copyright Act, Congress provided for a statutory right of the broadcaster to make the copy allowed in section 112(a), so that the broadcaster need not seek permission and a license each time they need a "server copy." [1] The right is conditioned upon the organization retaining and using it, and destroying the server copy within six months of the sound recording's first transmission to the public.

Despite Congress's provision for the broadcasting industry, however, the concept of a "server copy" is still a thorny issue for digital and online services.

WHY IS IT OKAY TO COPY MY MUSIC FROM COMPUTER TO MY PHONE, BUT I CAN'T SHARE IT?

Copyright protects covered works from unauthorized copying. When you move music files around, you are technically creating new copies of the music file onto the hard drive of your devices, and those copies are unauthorized unless specifically noted otherwise. So why don't music companies seem to care about this type of copying, when making a copy of the file for sharing has been so targeted?

The answer is somewhat murky. Technically, as long as you don't share the copy and you are creating a copy for personal use only, the RIAA seems to look the other way. Their website says such copying "won't usually raise concerns" if it's for personal use only, meaning that record labels seem less concerned about movement of personal copies than copies created and distributed, especially in today's streaming age. As evidenced by their lawsuits against individuals for Internet piracy, the labels' level of interest raises significantly if you start sharing those files.

---

1   *Copyright Act of 1976,* 17 U.S.C. § 112(e)

WHAT IS A "PERFORMANCE"?

In addition to a "copy," we have discussed the concept of a "public performance" as it applies to both musical works and sound recordings. Copyright law officially defines a public performance or display:

To perform or display a work publicly means:

- To perform or display it at a place open to the public or at any place where a substantial number of persons outside of a normal circle of a family and its social acquaintances is gathered; or

- To transmit or otherwise communicate a performance or display of the work to a place specified by clause (1) or to the public, by means of any device or process, whether the members of the public capable of receiving the performance or display receive it in the same place or in separate places and at the same time or at different times.

—Copyright Act of 1976, 17 U.S.C. § 101

Therefore, performance royalties can be derived by both live performances of musical compositions, as well as certain transmissions. This right is limited, however, depending on the type of copyright. Remember, sound recording copyright holders have only those rights under Copyright Act sections 106 (1), (2), (3), and (6), and there exists no right of public performance under section 106(4) for sound recordings.

A 2014 case decided by the Supreme Court, *ABC v. Aereo, Inc.*, found that a digital service that retransmitted broadcast television online was "publicly performing the works." The service had thousands of tiny antennas to capture broadcast television (one for each of its subscribers) and billed itself as a virtual "DVR" service. While the service and case did not have a specific music focus, it is an example of how "public performance" and other copyright concepts can be tested by new technologies and business models.

Streams and Downloads

As the distribution of music has moved online, questions have been raised about whether a stream is a performance or a download, or both, given that a data file must be downloaded into a computer's cache in order to play the stream on the computer. The Copyright Office considers a stream to qualify for performance and mechanical royalties, as confirmed by the rulings by the Copyright Royalty Board (and apparent approval by the Copyright Office) that set royalty rates for streaming and tethered downloads.

ASCAP and BMI have also argued that a permanent digital download also has a public performance royalty attached (and have lost in court so far). If read literally, however, the definition of "performance" includes the "transmission" of the work, and any download must technically be "transmitted" to the buyer. In Europe, rights holders have agreed to standards where a download ranges from 75–100 percent mechanical and 0–25 percent performance, with streams considered to be between 25–50 percent mechanical and 50–75 percent performance, all depending on territory. These questions and variations from country to country continue to highlight the ambiguity over how copyright should be applied online. We'll address these questions and how artists and writers get paid from digital performances starting in chapter 7.

CHAPTER 5

Musical Works

WRITERS AND PUBLISHERS: COPYRIGHT IN MUSIC PUBLISHING

It is often said that music publishing is "where the money is" in music. Despite troubled times for recorded music over the past two decades, many publishers have seen their revenue grow from other sources, such as performance and sync licensing, and often songwriters will choose to enter into a publishing deal for their musical compositions. These agreements allow publishers to monetize musical compositions, and come in a variety of shapes and sizes, including those for single songs and albums, as well as longer-term deals that provide an annual advance against royalties in exchange for delivery of a certain number of songs annually to the publisher. Beyond these factors, there are two fundamental types of publishing deals we'll discuss: a standard deal and co-publishing deal.

U.S. Publishing (NPMA) Industry Annual Revenues Breakdown

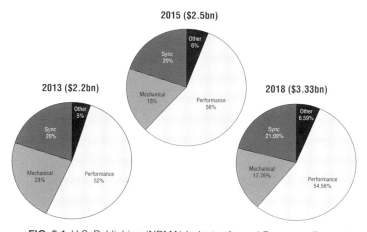

FIG. 5.1. U.S. Publishing (NPMA) Industry Annual Revenues Breakdown

In a standard publishing deal, the writer assigns 100 percent of the copyright in the musical composition to the publisher and receives 50 percent of the revenue. In a co-publishing deal, the writer transfers 50 percent of the copyright and retains 50 percent of the copyright and will receive 75 percent of the revenue. In a sense, because the writer has retained part of the copyright and is sharing the "publisher's share" of revenue, he or she is said to be also publishing the song (or "co-publishing" it with the publisher). Typically, only writers with some degree of leverage will be offered a co-publishing deal (i.e., they are already successful, or they are artist/writers with a major record deal where the publisher sees an already existing outlet for their works).

More established writers may choose to sign only an administration agreement, where the publisher merely issues licenses and collects royalties, in exchange for a 10 percent administration fee. The writer keeps 100 percent of his or her copyright in an administration deal.

There are other considerations for a publishing deal too. Writers should ask for their royalties to be paid "at-source," with no deductions for foreign subpublishing fees. (*Subpublishers* are publishers in foreign countries who will collect in those territories on behalf of a publisher.) Be sure your publisher is paying you a part of an advance received specifically related to your music. You should also consider asking for a reversion of your copyright after a period of time, or upon meeting some financial threshold.

I WAS OFFERED A PUBLISHING DEAL, BUT I OFTEN HEAR THAT I SHOULD SELF-PUBLISH. HOW DO I DECIDE WHAT TO DO?

It really depends on your situation. Some writers may choose to sign a publishing deal because they believe the publisher can significantly help with placements of their material and drive royalties that they could not otherwise generate on their own. Others may need the royalty advance for living expenses (or as a way of leveraging future income, in the case of already successful writers). If you are already successful and have outlets for your material, it may be in your best interest to sign an administration deal only, where the publisher merely collects the royalties and handles paperwork on your behalf.

Writer/Publisher Splits and Shares

Perhaps one of the most confusing things about music publishing is the concept of shares. As we saw above, typically in a standard publishing deal, the publisher owns 100 percent of the copyright, but is entitled to only 50 percent of the royalty payments, paying the other 50 percent to the writer, after deducting expenses approved in the agreement and any advances already paid to the writer.

	Standard Publishing Deal	Co-Publishing Deal	Admin Deal
Copyright Ownership	Publisher: 100% Writer: 0%	Publisher: 50% Writer: 50%	Publisher: 0% Writer: 100%
Royalty Split	Publisher: 50% Writer: 50%	Publisher: 25% Writer: 75%	Publisher: 10% Writer: 90%

FIG. 5.2. Royalty Shares

At a PRO, each song usually has two accounts tied to it: the publisher account and the writer account, and each is said to have its "share" (i.e., its portion of the profits). Therefore, in a co-publishing deal, the writer is "sharing" or "co-publishing" and receiving half of what the publisher gets in a standard publishing deal. We should remember that *the writer's share of public performance royalties from a PRO is **always** paid directly to the writer and **never** to the publisher, meaning it can't be used for recoupment of publishing advances.*

HOW DO I START MY OWN PUBLISHING COMPANY?

To begin to publish your music, you'll need to first form a publishing company with your desired PRO. You can do this by filing an application to affiliate with ASCAP, BMI, SESAC, or GMR (remember that the last two are by invitation only). Your application will require you to suggest some name possibilities. Once you have your confirmed affiliation and name, which could take up to two months, you can file for a fictitious name registration in your state (if you're going to do business as yourself individually) or file for an LLC or corporation to manage the works. Once these steps are complete, you should register the copyrights on the works you own, as well as ensuring they are properly registered with your selected PRO. You should also register your works with the MLC in order to collect your mechanical royalties.

Key Terms to Know in a Publishing Agreement:

administration: services such as registering copyrights, issuing licenses, collecting monies, and making payments to writers

advance: a prepayment of royalties which can be recouped later from royalty earnings

at source: royalties are paid to the writer based on the income received in the "source country"

blanket license: a license by a copyright user for a group of songs in exchange for a single fee (think of a radio station that pays a single fee to BMI for all of its repertoire)

bundles: a combination of products, like a download along with the purchase of a CD

catch-all: a term used to describe all other income not specifically called out in a publishing agreement

collection period: a post-term period of a publishing agreement during which the publisher can continue to collect monies owed during the term (usually 1–2 years)

controlled composition: a song that is "controlled" by an artist— usually by writing it or owning part of the copyright

co-publishing: a type of publishing deal where the writer is considered a "co-publisher" and entitled to half of the typical "publisher's share"

cover recordings: a recording by an artist who is not the original songwriter

cross-collateralization (or *"crossed"*): the ability of a music company to recoup or aggregate royalties from multiple agreements instead of only the single agreement at hand

escalation: an increase in royalty rates when a songwriter reaches a certain threshold (usually revenue-based)

grand rights: the right to use a song in a play, or audiovisual work, but only if the song is integrated into the story being told

initial period: the first, guaranteed period of the contract

letter of direction: a letter signed by the songwriter directing a third party to do something on his/her behalf (usually to pay royalties or revenue to a certain person)

mechanical fees: fees for the reproduction of the musical composition (this can be as a physical sale, download, or stream)

MDR (*minimum delivery requirement*): the specified minimum number of songs a writer must deliver under a publishing agreement

performance fees: fees for the public performance of a song

pipeline income: income received by publisher but not yet accounted to the songwriter

renewal (or *option*) *period*: periods of the contract after the Initial Period, often contingent on a milestone or threshold, but occasionally auto-renewing

retention period: the post-term period during which the publisher still has rights to a song before any reversion

reversion: the return of the copyright ownership in a song to the writer, usually upon some threshold

royalty: the percentage of revenue from a song paid to the writer from the publisher

sampling: the use of a sound within another work. If the underlying musical work is played in the studio as part of a new, larger recording, it may be referred to as a "replay"

statutory rate: the rate set by law for the reproduction of a musical composition in a sound recording

subpublisher: a publisher in a foreign territory who collects on behalf of your publisher, and typically takes a fee of around 15-25% before sending the funds to your publisher

synchronization license: a license granted to "synchronize" the musical work with audiovisual images, typically from television, film, advertising

term: the total duration of the contract

territory: the regions of the world covered by the contract

transcription license: a license granted to use the musical work with other audio, such as radio advertising and podcasts

unallocated guarantee or advance payment: a flat fee received by a publisher for the use of its repertoire that is not allocated for a single songwriter or song

Administration Resources (PROs, HFA, and Beyond)

Licensing of musical works can be a painful, tedious process. Fortunately the MMA and MLC have somewhat simplified the process for mechanical royalties. Publishers and writers can now choose to license through entities like MRI or HFA, or to use the MLC's services. The PROs are unavoidable if a musical composition owner wants to collect public performance royalties from all radio stations, live venues, and online services. In another example of a changing market with changing market forces, some publishers in the U.S. have attempted to withdraw their "digital" rights from the PROs and license the rights themselves to obtain a higher royalty rate, a move which was struck down by rate courts who can review the consent decrees under which BMI and ASCAP operate. The court stated in the ASCAP case (which was the result of a dispute with Pandora), that publishers are "all-in" unless they resign from ASCAP completely:

> "Because the language of the consent decree unambiguously requires ASCAP to provide Pandora with a license to perform all of the works in its repertory, and because ASCAP retains the works of 'withdrawing' publishers in its repertory even if it purports to lack the right to license them to a subclass of New Media entities, Pandora's motion for summary judgment is granted."[1]

The BMI judge separately decided that publishers are "all out" if they have withdrawn new media rights from BMI. It is important to remember that publishers can still directly license their works to digital services, because PROs have *non-exclusive* rights to license their repertoire, and the digital service can then claim a pro rata reduction (equivalent to the value of the catalogues directly licensed) in the license fee paid to the PRO.

A Global Review: Musical Works Licensing in the U.S. and Beyond

As discussed in chapter 2, there are some substantial differences between the U.S. system for licensing and those of foreign countries. One notable distinction is that in many countries, mechanical royalties and public performance royalties are collected by the same organization. In most territories, mechanical licenses are a percentage of revenue, as opposed to the "penny rate" system in the U.S. (9.1 cents per song). There is also what is called a "neighboring right," which is the full performance rights in sound recordings (in

---

1   In re Petition of Pandora Media, Inc. Related to *U.S. v. ASCAP* (S.D.N.Y. 2013).

territories that are signatories to the Rome Convention and others that have adopted them. While many industrialized nations are signatories to the Rome Convention, the U.S. is not, but neighboring rights exist for digital transmissions in the U.S., as we've already discussed.) Several companies are now offering a service to collect your overseas neighboring rights money by directly affiliating with the in-country society that manages it, and can bring a significant new revenue stream. Left uncollected, the cash is eventually distributed to performers in the territory (who have no real right to it!).

MY MUSIC ISN'T VERY POPULAR IN MY HOME COUNTRY, BUT I'VE LEARNED IT'S A HUGE HIT IN SEVERAL OTHER COUNTRIES. HOW DO I COLLECT MY ROYALTIES FOR THIS?

If you are a writer and member of a PRO in the U.S., they should be collecting public performance royalties from other foreign collecting societies for you. A publisher should have a sub-publisher to collect mechanical royalties from foreign territories, as well. If you own your own rights, this is a more tedious process, as you'll need to create these relationships on your own, but it's possible to set up your own accounts with foreign PROs for your works. For neighboring rights, if you meet the eligibility conditions, some companies are now offering collection services from foreign collecting societies. Be sure you are staying on top of all of these rights.

The Basics of EU Copyright and Music

In the European Union, copyright is guided by EU directives that dictate to member states how to act on copyright, but the law is still promulgated on a country-by-country basis. The overall regime protects copying, distribution, public performances, fixation, rental, and provides for a copyright duration of life plus 70 years after the death of the last remaining author for written works, and 70 years after publication or communication to the public of a performance and of a sound recording. An open-ended fair use defense like that in the U.S. does not exist in the EU, but member states are free to choose exceptions for which a use cannot be considered infringing.

Temporary copying is authorized for purposes of electronic communication in the EU, and authors and performers have moral rights. Recent directives have brought cross border licen-sing through collective licensing organizations (administering both mechanical and public performance rights). Until 2019, there was a safe harbor for ISPs (like the DMCA in the U.S., which we'll discuss in more detail later) and companies providing hosting services, and prevention of content security circumvention. Mechanical royalties are licensed as a percentage of revenue. For public performances, musical compositions and sound recordings are licensed through collective licensing organizations, with sound recordings usually on a compulsory basis. Contractual standards developed by PROs make sure that authors and lyricists retain 50 percent of their mechanical and public performance rights payments (as opposed to 0 percent for mechanical rights in the U.S. under standard deals).

The EU has also adopted a "making available" right, based on WIPO treaties. In 1996, WIPO finalized the WCT and WPPT, commonly referred to as the WIPO Internet Treaties. As part of these changes, WIPO required its treaty signatories to give copyright owners an exclusive right to:

> *"authorize any communication to the public of their works, by wire or wireless means, including making available to the public of their works in such a way that members of the public may access these works from a place and at a time individually chosen by them."*

EU copyright law has very specifically implemented this concept, arguing that the "making available" right includes scenarios where the consumer does not actually avail themselves of the available work. Separately, while the U.S. updated copyright to comply with the WCT and WPPT under the Digital Millennium Copyright Act in 1998, it did not specifically amend the law to offer a "making available" right. The argument in the U.S. has traditionally been that the "making available" right is encompassed in the exclusive rights to control copying, distribution, and public performance.

2019 EU DIRECTIVE ON COPYRIGHT IN THE DIGITAL SINGLE MARKET

In 2019, the European Union adopted a new directive on copyright. The most substantive change for music came with the closure of the "safe harbor" provision that allowed user-generated content companies like YouTube and Soundcloud to avoid copyright infringement liability as long as they complied with certain measures, like taking down content on the request of the copyright owner. These services are now required to have a license for any material they make available. There are some exceptions for small-scale services.

CHAPTER 6

Sound Recordings

As detailed in chapter 1, the distribution medium of choice for music has evolved dramatically since music was first recordable in the late 1800s. By far, the most phenomenal shift in distribution of music came with the wide adoption of the Internet in the past fifteen years. First taking off in the late 1990s, in association with illegal sites such as the original Napster, online distribution of music has flourished.

Furthermore, as times have changed, there are now multiple options for artists to release their recorded music and benefit from their sound recording copyright (as opposed to their musical composition copyright). "Traditional" record deals still exist, with all of their complexities (we'll discuss those in a second), but most have added "all-rights" or "360" provisions, which allow the label to collect percentages of non-recorded music revenue, like touring, merchandise, and publishing. However, so-called "do-it-yourself" (DIY) has also taken off with the disruption of distribution models, and all artists are expected to have done some basic legwork to promote themselves before attracting interest from large publishers and labels, which are interested in the number of streams and "likes" an artist can show.

The traditional record label model still requires that the artist give full copyright ownership to the label, and consists of upfront money to an artist (usually in the form of an advance payment against future royalties) and payment of recording costs for an album (collectively, their "advance"). These costs are recouped from the artist's royalties, but are not considered a loan and an artist can never be sued for money owed on his/her royalty account. A new artist may start at around a 13 to 15 percent royalty, while established sellers may garner close to 20 percent. But, this is 15 percent of what? (One of the first things to investigate with any record deal is whether royalties are paid on wholesale [also known as PPD, published price to dealer], or suggested retail price, and how licenses to digital services and others are handled.)

Labels then may take some deductions from the royalty accounts:

1. a packaging deduction of usually 25 percent (a leftover from the days of CDs)

2. a "free goods" deduction of 15 percent, usually only on physical product, and resulting from a legacy label practice of only charging a retailer for 85 of the 100 pieces of product delivered

3. a "promotional copy" deduction of 10 percent, again, now only on physical product (since there is no incremental cost to creating an additional digital file)

4. a "reserve for returns" of up to 35 percent, allocating a percentage to hold back in the event the record is returned (there is no reserve for returns on digital sales since there is no hard copy to be returned).

Labels typically then charge back other out-of-pocket costs to artists, such as costs of making videos (50 percent recoupable) and third-party out-of-pocket costs (also 50 percent recoupable). Other revenue sources from licensing the sound recording are also typically credited to an artist's account at a 50 percent royalty. (There have been many disputes about this in recent years, with Eminem's team winning a court decision that payments for digital sales (characterized as licenses) under his 1990s era recording agreement should be at 50 percent instead of the lower "sale" royalty rate Universal had been paying. The effect of the case was millions of dollars in additional royalties to Eminem over a decade.)

Royalties are also "all-in," meaning that producer advances are paid out of artist royalties. Royalty clauses in recording agreements often have *escalations* as well, which pay higher percentages once the artist achieves a certain level of sales. Finally, many recording agreements have "controlled composition" clauses, which state that any *musical works* owned or controlled by the *artist* are licensed to the record label at 75 percent of the compulsory mechanical license rate (the 9.1 cent rate we discussed earlier). There is also usually a maximum amount of mechanical license payments the label will pay (10 times 75 percent of the standard rate). In a world of streaming, where mechanical license revenue is paid directly by the service to the musical composition rights owner, this clause is becoming less relevant.

In the mid 2000s, major labels began to insist upon all-rights (commonly referred to as "360") record deals, where they also take a percentage of other artist revenue, such as touring, merchandising, and publishing. Percentages vary widely (3 to 30 percent) and exceptions are often carved out (for example, no payment on publishing if the artist is also signed to the publishing division of the parent company of the record label). The justification for these all-rights deals is that labels spend enormous amounts of money marketing artists, therefore opening the doors for them to these other revenue streams. Significant outcry at the outset has somewhat faded, and 360 provisions are very typical today.

Beyond the traditional record deal, another type of record deal, more common with independent labels, is a "net-profits" deal for an artist who already has a recorded album ready to be released. In this arrangement, the album is licensed to the label for exclusive distribution for some set period of time (usually five to ten years). The parties will deduct third party expenses from the revenue brought in by the album and then "split the profits" 50/50.

Record deals often have a number of other provisions, such as:

1. a re-recording restriction (you can't re-record a song on the album for a certain period of time);

2. that the material is "commercially satisfactory" (i.e. market viable in the eyes of the label);

3. that the album is not a live album, or instrumental.

If you are an artist, be sure to request a "pay-or-play" provision, which is essentially a commitment by the record label to release your album or pay a penalty. For example, they may have six months after you turn in the master recordings to release it, or they will give you the rights to the master recordings as a penalty if they fail to do so. This prevents you from being in the untenable situation of recording an album for two years, only to never have it see the light of day. You should also look for an "audit" clause, which allows you to check the accounting of the label when they make royalty payments to you.

Finally, some independents have an "upstream" arrangement with a major label, where the major will take over the marketing and promotion of the artist's album once a certain level of sales and/or digital consumption takes place and pay a royalty to the smaller label.

SAMPLE ROYALTY CALCULATION

Let's take a look at a sample royalty calculation:

Recording fund advance:	$200,000
Royalty rate on wholesale (PPD):	15%
Controlled compositions/mechanical royalties:	75% (10 song max)
Free goods (hard goods):	15%
Packaging deduction (includes digital):	25%
Promotional copies (hard goods):	10%
Video	Recoupable at 50%
Other licenses	Royalty of 50%

Let's say download sales generate $600,000 in PPD revenue.
CDs and vinyl generate $200,000 in PPD revenue (10 tracks per disc, 20,000 sold at $10).
They sell one master-use license for film at $20,000.

What is the artist owed?
  Royalty rate on downloads = 15% * 75% = real royalty rate of 11.25%
  Royalty rate on hard goods = 15% * 75% * 85% * 90% = real royalty rate of 8.6%

  Artist spent $150,000 to record album, and $50,000 on a video.

  So, artist would receive:

11.25%* $600,000	=	$67,500
8.6%* $200,000	=	$17,200
50% of $20,000	=	$10,000
Total Income:	=	**$94,700**

  Artist is owed $94,700, but his royalty account started off –$280,280:
$200,000 advance and $25,000 in video costs (50%), minus also mechanical royalties 9.1 cents * 75% = 6.91 cents * 800,000 tracks = $55,280.
  So, his current account is –**$205,830**
  What if you've already recorded your album, and you'd just like to work with an independent label to get it released and promoted to the public? Another type of deal, the "net-profits" deal, may be a better option for you. Under this concept, a label will take an exclusive license to your sound recordings (no ownership of copyright) for a period of time, usually five to ten years, at which point all rights revert to you. The label will then split equally with you all

profits from the sale of the recordings, after the expenses of the sale (but the recording costs you've already incurred are not included, meaning they'll have to be covered by your 50 percent of the profits).

Let's take a look at this calculation:

- Artist spent $50,000 on recording costs
- 7-year license to XXX Records
- 50/50 profit split after third-party expenses

- Sells $150,000 in iTunes download sales
- Streaming royalties equal $5,000
- Spends $10,000 on an outside publicist, mechanicals are full rate ($9,100)

So, the artist is owed $150,000 * .70 (because wholesale on iTunes is 70%) + $5,000 in streaming revenue − $10,000 − $9,100 = $90,900/2 = **$45,450**. But remember, he spent $50,000 on recording!!!

If you are an artist or songwriter with multiple publishing and recording deals, watch out for attempts to "cross-collateralize" the deals, meaning the label or publisher can recoup advances and costs from royalties not just under the agreement that provided for the advances, but from any other deal between their company and the writer/artist. You may be hundreds of thousands of dollars in the red as an artist on one early record deal, and later become a star songwriter signed to the publishing arm of the record label. It's in your best interest to ensure the label isn't taking your publishing royalties to pay back negative recording royalty accounts.

Finally, don't forget that in a digital world, self-distribution is also an option. Companies like Tunecore and CDBaby allow you to get your music on digital services like Apple Music and Spotify for a small fee, but remember that just because your music is available doesn't mean people are listening. (There are millions of never-before-streamed tracks on Spotify today; check out forgotify.com!) You'll need a comprehensive plan to market your album and get your music heard (getting on a playlist alone may generate thousands of dollars in streaming income), and there are many companies now offering "label services," such as Kobalt/AWAL and Thirty Tigers, that may be able to help you with this.

Key Terms to Know in a Recording Agreement:

360 rights: rights of a record company to share in all artist revenue (like a 360 degree circle)

advance: a prepayment of royalties which can be recouped later from royalty earnings

all-in: the total royalty paid by the record label including any producer or other royalties

ARPU (average revenue per user): the average amount of revenue received by a streaming service from each user on the platform

at source: royalties are paid to the record company based on the income received in the "source country"

bundles: a combination of products, like a download along with the purchase of a CD

ceiling: maximum advance in a subsequent period using a formula

commercially satisfactory: recordings which have the potential to be successful

controlled composition clause: a reduced mechanical royalty to be paid for Controlled Compositions of the artist

cross-collateralization (or *"crossed"*): the ability of a music company to recoup or aggregate royalties from multiple agreements instead of only the single agreement at hand

escalation: an increase in royalty rates when a record reaches a certain threshold (usually revenue or sales-based)

floor: minimum advance in a subsequent period using a formula

formula: a pre-determined calculation of the next period's advance based on prior album success

free goods: promotional products given away to retailers by record labels, and often a deduction is taken in the royalties accounting for these

fund (recording fund): the total advance to be paid to an artist, which includes any amounts for recording and other costs

initial period: the first, guaranteed period of the contract

letter of direction: a letter signed by an artist or producer directing a third party to do something on his/her behalf (usually to pay royalties or revenue to a certain person)

master: the recording

matching right: a right of first refusal on one or more rights of an artist

MDR (*minimum delivery requirement*): the specified minimum number of albums a writer must deliver under a publishing agreement

net artist rate: the royalty rate received by an artist after producer and other royalties are paid from the all-in royalty

pay-or-play (*release commitment*): a release commitment requiring a record label to either release your record or pay a penalty

PPD (*published price to dealer*): the wholesale price paid by a retailer to the record label

promotional copies: copies given away to radio stations and reviewers (less relevant as the world becomes fully digital)

recoupment: retaining royalties to repay an artist advance

renewal (or *option*) *period*: periods of the contract after the Initial Period, often contingent on a milestone or threshold, but occasionally auto-renewing

reserves: a holdback of royalty payments on some percentage due to the possibility of returned merchandise

reversion: the return of the copyright ownership in masters to the artist, usually upon some threshold

royalty: the percentage of revenue from a recording paid to the artist by the record label

sampling: the use of a sound within another work

scale: the minimum amount a union requires to be paid to its member (typically reference for studio musicians)

streaming equivalent album (*SEA*): the stream of a song 1,500 times, deemed to be the sale of an album

term: the total duration of the contract

territory: the regions of the world covered by the contract

tour support: additional funds given to an artist by a record label to make up for tour losses (usually recoupable)

track equivalent album (*TEA*): the sale of 10 single-song downloads, deemed to be the sale of an album

CHAPTER 7

Touring and Artist Management

While the subject of this book is copyright and recorded music, no discussion of the music industry would be relevant without a short look at touring and artist management, particularly when all-rights deals are blending the responsibilities and payment streams. Meanwhile, Live Nation, the world's largest concert promoter, now owns the largest artist management company in the U.S., Artist Nation.

I'VE BEEN APPROACHED BY SEVERAL ARTIST MANAGERS, BUT THEY ALL WANT ME TO SIGN A LONG-TERM CONTRACT. WHAT IF THEY DON'T DEVELOP MY CAREER SUCCESSFULLY?

If you are an artist and are signing a contract with a new artist manager, be sure your lawyer negotiates milestones into your contract, which if not met, will allow you to fire the manager and move on with your career. For example, if the manager does not get you a major label record deal in the first two years, or you do not achieve some minimum level of total revenue before costs ($50 0,000/$1,000,000/$2,000,000) as an artist in the first three years, you'll be able to terminate the agreement. This ensures your manager is incentivized to work for you. But, be aware that generally, managers anticipate that it will take three years of work to properly develop an artist's career.

As an artist's career develops, he or she will be thrust into a world of managers and agents who want to help them, in exchange for a percentage of earnings. In theory, this is a great arrangement, as interests are aligned and they are compensated for making the artist successful. Agents typically take 10 percent of the gross revenue of any employment contract they secure (sponsorship, live performance, etc.). Live music promoters will contract with the agent for the artist's performance, pay usually a 50 percent deposit, and often ask for a "radius clause," which is a contractual commitment that the artist won't play again in a certain region for a certain period of time before and after the contracted concert.

Artist managers in the U.S. typically take 15 to 25 percent of gross revenue, but gross revenue is often up for discussion in the contract. Is the manager taking care of your affairs in the entertainment industry, or just music? This would impact the manager's ability to commission money made from a movie. Also, is the manager entitled to commission your music publishing earnings, or only those you earn as an artist? What about tour support and recording advances from your label? A lawyer can help to ensure all of this is clear.

Next, in the event the artist/manager relationship does end at some point, many managers demand what is known as a "sunset clause," the right to post-term commission. As we noted, managers often do a lot of work for a long period of time to make an artist successful, and they are often looking over their shoulder for another manager who wants to take on their artist just as he/she becomes successful. At a minimum, managers should be paid commission on all agreements they've negotiated for the artist, and with a sunset clause, may be entitled a percentage of gross revenue in the years after the relationship ends. For example, a manager might receive 15 percent in the first year, 10 percent in the second, and 5 percent in the third year after the artist-manager contract ends.

Other important legal clauses to know in artist management agreements include a "limited power of attorney," allowing the manager to sign business deals in the artist's stead when the artist is not available, and milestones that the manager might need to meet in order to keep the contract continuing (see sidebar). You may also want a "key man" clause, which requires the manager to continue to actively personally manage you or allow you to terminate the relationship if he fails to do so for more than thirty days. This prevents artists from ending up at a large management company if their manager sells his firm, assigns his contracts, and then leaves the larger company for some reason.

MY PERSONAL MANAGER WANTS A POWER OF ATTORNEY, BUT HE'S NOT MY LAWYER. WHAT DOES HE MEAN?

A power of attorney allows someone else (not necessarily a lawyer) to sign on your behalf. In this case, your manager probably wants to be able to sign touring and other fairly standard agreements for you while you are on tour, making the logistics of finalizing such deals easier on both him/her and you. Be sure the power is "limited" only to deals similar to those you've already agreed to in the past, and that the manager should endeavor to contact you first for verbal approval.

Remember that these are some guidelines only, and many artist managers work only on handshake deals with their artists, theorizing that if the artist isn't happy, they should be free to go since they'll be difficult to manage anyway.

Key Terms to Know in Management, Agency, and Touring Agreements:

commission: a percentage of your earnings owed to a manager or agent as their compensation

key man clause: allows the artist to terminate the contract if his/her key relationship with the management firm or agency leaves the company

loan-out firm: a corporation or limited liability company formed by an artist (for liability protections) who then "provides" the services of the artist

sunset clause: post-term commission for contracts entered into during the contract

term: the duration of the contract

territory: the regions of the world where you are represented

CHAPTER 8

Copyright and the Changing Distribution of Music

There is little question that music's grand entrance to online distribution and the Internet era generally, years ago, was an unlawful one. The ushering parties, Napster and other peer-to-peer or "P2P" sites, made it extremely easy and cheap (free) for online users to acquire and consume music often without a trace, and in almost all cases, without compensating the copyright owners for the protected uses of their works.

In response to the overwhelming growth of piracy, the RIAA sued individual file sharers, and copyright holders have sued the companies providing the mechanisms that enable file sharing online. At least two of the notable court cases that came as a result have helped to shape our understanding of legal distribution of music online. Specifically, the Napster and Grokster cases (decided in 2001 and 2005, respectively) helped to define what is and is not permitted online. You can read more about these cases in chapter 11.

While these two cases were making their way through the judicial system, a number of legal music services were developing their own legal services. Among them was Apple, which was confident in the role it would play in the music industry. Armed with content license deals with the (then) five major record labels amounting to a 200,000+ track-strong library, Apple had a public goal of selling one million tracks within one month when it was launched in 2003. Over the past decade, Apple sold billions of tracks, but jumped into the streaming game with Apple Music after seeing its download sales decline while subscription-based services like Spotify and TIDAL shifted total recorded music revenue to an access model instead of sales.

Global Recorded Music Industry Revenues 2001–2018 (US$ Billions)

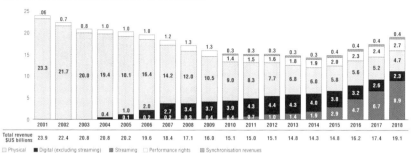

FIG. 8.1. Global Recorded Music Industry Revenues 2005–2015 (US$ Billions)

Today, global digital revenue now exceeds physical sales, but in many markets, physical sales are still dominant.[1] Germany, for example, still derives 60 percent of its recorded music revenue from physical product, while on the opposite side, Sweden's market is predominantly digital, and a whopping 92 percent of that digital market is subscription services. In 2019, music subscription revenue was almost $9B globally, growing by more than 30 percent in a year. Goldman Sachs projects recorded music revenues of $40b in 2030, excluding publishing.[2] Spotify and others offer tens of millions of tracks available for instantaneous streaming; however, curation and discovery remain intractable issues in the emerging models, and as mentioned earlier, approximately one quarter of the music on Spotify has never been streamed.

Regardless of where one falls in the industry—a record label executive, an artist, a startup in the entertainment space, a songwriter— the changing models of digital sales and distribution will continue to shape the industry and market as we know them. So, how does one succeed—or even survive—in this quickly evolving field of creation, practice, or business?

Getting to the bottom of some fundamental questions is a good start for any rights holder, creator, businessperson, or visionary seeking to survive and thrive in the current market. How is music distributed online? How do artists, labels, music publishers, and digital distributors get paid? How can one control distribution of their works

1   *Digital Music Report*, IFPI, 2016
2   *Music in the Air*, Goldman Sachs, 2020

on the Internet? Is it still possible to make a living in the music business despite the incredible losses due to online piracy and low per-stream rates? What about the greater transparency that should be brought by digital streaming, which is completely trackable and reportable?

Although imperfect in its application and certainly wrought with flaws, copyright law and the businesses that depend on its enforcement have generally adapted to accommodate innovations in the music business.

However, while Congress has tried to anticipate future delivery schemes for music and other copyrighted works, wholesale rewrites to copyright law cannot occur on a dime. Distribution models and payment schemes change nearly every year to accompany transforming technologies and a continuous stream of new offerings. And as we have seen so far, a number of various stakeholders are affected, and each must appropriately implement measures to ensure compliance with any new copyright legislation.

COPYRIGHT LAW AND THE RINGTONE

The growing popularity of ringtones in the mid 2000s highlighted gaps in copyright definitions. Copyright law provided for a statutory mechanical license rate of 9.1 cents per copy of a composition embodied in a track delivered or sold. (This rate is adjusted for inflation from time to time, usually every two to three years.) However, this was not a good fit with the ringtone market, as ringtones are typically sold at a premium and do not embody an entire composition. Naturally, with the raging popularity of these products (which became a multi-billion dollar industry in less than a decade, and then promptly dropped off again), the numerous stakeholders were tireless in their efforts to arrive at an appropriate rate.

At the outset, publishers were typically receiving up to 10 percent of the retail price for the sale of a ringtone, which could vary wildly depending on the sale price. In 2006, the Copyright Office ruled that ringtones were subject to the compulsory mechanical license, which for digital phonorecords is the established flat rate of 9.1 cents. Naturally, publishers were not pleased with this outcome.

In 2008, the Copyright Royalty Board established statutory rates for the reproduction of musical compositions as part of the sale or distribution of ringtones at 24 cents. Needless to say, this was quite a victory for music publishers. The dispute is representative of an industry that must make up new rules as technology changes the landscape.

Another deficiency often decried by online music providers has been the lack of comprehensive clearinghouse for mechanical licenses online. Until recently, this left music services in the unpleasant and costly position of having to negotiate separately with each of the remaining publishers for each musical composition offered on their services. The MMA has sought to solve this with the development of the MLC, offering blanket licenses to DSPs and songwriters and copyright owners a place to claim royalties. The reform was much needed and supported by the entire value chain, from publishers to DSPs.

Going even further, the Copyright Office has recommended development of a music rights organization that can license all-rights, instead of just performance or just mechanical rights. The Office released a comprehensive report in 2015 that recommended:

1. The concept of Music Rights Organizations (entities that can license more than one set of rights at once—for example, mechanical and performance royalties).

2. A full public performance right in sound recordings. This would offer another revenue stream and bring the U.S. into line with the rest of the world, also allowing U.S. artists to tap into foreign performance royalties (neighboring rights), which are not currently paid due to the lack of reciprocity in the U.S.

3. Review of the ASCAP and BMI Consent Decrees, and the ability for musical works owners to negotiate the rates for their music on a fair market basis, like the sound recording copyright owners already do.

4. Private sector help in creating a registry or database of copyrighted works.

Finally, the lawsuit by ASCAP seeking a public performance right in a download further illustrates the difficulties posed by antiquated laws that are often interpreted to the benefit of each reader. Rights holders continue to seek more revenue as a result of the ambiguity of the law applied to emerging distribution methods, leading primarily to a windfall for lawyers, rather than copyright owners. One of the prevailing practices for new online businesses has been to start a service that may or may not be legal under current law, attract a significant user base, get sued, and use the user base as leverage in negotiations to obtain legitimate license from rights owners, with SoundCloud in 2015 as the most recent example of a popular service to go "legal."

Further complicating matters are the logistical hurdles that stand in the way of copyright reform. Often, legislation is held up in committee or not passed due to the efforts of lobbyists with opposing interests. For example, we have moved from an era of sales of music (when radio was considered to be promotional for record sales) to an era of access, and many would argue that a "listen" on AM/FM is the same as a "listen" on Pandora or Spotify. Yet the radio broadcasters lobbying group is considered to be among the largest and most powerful in Washington, and they have defeated every attempt to date to assign a full performance right to sound recordings, which could result in significant new revenue for labels and artists when their music is played on AM/FM radio.

We will now shift into diving deeper into music law in the digital context of our era. Specifically, we will summarize the current distribution channels and mediums and how they interact with U.S. copyright law. We'll also explore current and future business models for music distribution via online and mobile channels. With this analysis, we'll also assist in identifying where copyright law has failed us in providing a suitable framework for rights allocation and associated royalties. Last but not least, we'll apply some of these considerations to the international context: how do these rights translate across borders? All in all, you will be equipped with a vocabulary and deeper understanding of how the current system works, and is likely to work, in years to come. Let's examine the current offerings and business models available.

WHO IS MAKING MONEY IN THE "DIGITAL MUSIC INDUSTRY"?

Who is making money in "digital music"? For a long time, the mainstream answer was quite simple: Apple. But while Apple prevails as the best-known success story in recent years, its revenues do not stem from music sales or music distribution of any kind. Apple's fiscal and brand success is a direct result of its phenomenal hardware sales, specifically the Mac and the iPhone, and music is a tiny piece of their revenue. The same theory holds true for Google, which has built a tremendous business making money on advertising by helping users locate content, but does not actually pay for the content.

This has led some to debate the so-called "transfer of value" in the internet economy—the idea that technology companies like Apple, Google, and Facebook, as well as ISPs like Verizon and Comcast, are enriching their business and profits by delivering copyrighted content for which they pay little or nothing under current copyright law.

That argument aside, the area of interest and opportunity in the industry lies in emerging business models for the distribution and consumption of music and a range of music-related products. After years of fighting online piracy and restricting new business models offered by companies such as RealNetworks, Yahoo, YouTube, and others, music rights holders (record labels and music publishers) seem to be finally coming around and supporting the innovation needed to sustain their revenues. As subscription grows, a number of new initiatives by rights holders are showing increased creati-vity and a desire to make the rules of the game, rather than playing someone else's. As an example, labels now have equity positions in many streaming services. Major labels made large profits from the initial public offering of Spotify in 2018 due to their ownership stakes. According to press information, their artists and songwriters were paid a share of these profits based on usage and breakage (overflow payment) policies.

CHAPTER 9

Digital Music Delivery Formats

As we have seen, the music business derives income from a variety of rights that entitle copyright holders to a plethora of assorted revenue streams. Going online, depending on the delivery format, different copyrights are implicated with different rates, and different rights holders or administrators are paid accordingly. This chapter will describe the four mainstream digital music delivery formats and explain the copyright licensing implications for each. (Note that illegal P2P offerings are not addressed here. Services such as BitTorrent operate by facilitating a connection between two individual users who wish to "share" their files. This section concerns legitimate, legal distribution of music done with the consent of the associated rights holders.)

	Permanent Downloads	Conditional Downloads	On-Demand Streaming	Internet Radio
Sound Recording Rights	Wholesale rates are negotiated with each label/licensor; typically per track/album	Variable rates are negotiated with each label/licensor; typically per play or revenue share	Variable rates are negotiated with each label/licensor; typically per play or revenue share	Compulsory rates typically paid to Sound-Exchange (generally on a per-performance basis)
Reproduction Right/Mechanical	Compulsory Rate: 9.1 cents per track or 1.75 cents/minute	Gradually increasing to 15.1% of service revenue in 2022, minus PRO fees (under appeal as of this writing)	Gradually increasing to 15.1% of service revenue in 2022, minus PRO fees (under appeal as of this writing)	None
Public Performance Right	None, as there is no public performance attributed to downloads in the U.S.	None, per recent decisions, as there is no public performance attributable to a conditional download	Yes, negotiated with each PRO	Yes, negotiated with each PRO

FIG. 9.1. Licensing Models for Various Digital Music Offerings

PERMANENT DOWNLOADS

Permanent downloads are also known as "tracks," "MP3s," and "downloads."

Functionality

Permanent downloads are tracks or songs that are delivered via the Internet and can be stored and played from digital music or MP3 players, mobile phones, a computer's hard drive, a compact disc, etc. Permanent downloads are generally purchased from online stores in a format superior to what one typically finds on a P2P site, typically with a higher bit rate and no imperfections. Companies that sell permanent downloads include iTunes, Rhapsody, and Amazon. Formats vary.

Many of the download stores began years ago by selling tracks with digital rights management features (DRM). Often required by record labels, DRM functioned to limit the end users' ability to copy the file, among other things. In 2008, several popular online stores, including iTunes, Amazon, and Rhapsody, prevailed in obtaining licenses from record labels that allowed them to distribute permanent downloads "DRM-free," as MP3s. This long-awaited shift allowed users to play downloads on a broader range of hardware—most importantly, iPods and iPhones. Until late 2008, Apple had refused to sell tracks without its proprietary DRM or license its technology to others, which limited the interoperability of various stores' content and hardware devices, but a potential EU antitrust investigation likely impacted its decision-making process.

Business Model

The business model for permanent downloads is simple, generally. Closest of all online models to the physical model, online distributors pay a wholesale rate for tracks/albums and control retail pricing themselves, keeping the margin as a small profit.

From the launch of its iTunes store in 2003 until early 2009, Apple maintained the standard fee for online track sales with the vast majority of online tracks selling for $.99 each. The iTunes store now sells tracks and albums with varied pricing schemes for track downloads at the behest of labels and in exchange for dropping DRM.

COST PER TRACK

Perhaps as a result of distributor-side marketing research, or perhaps as a result of pressure from record labels, in late 2008 and early 2009, the major download retail stores started to adjust their retail prices for track sales. Instead of all tracks selling for $.99, the stores are now selling tracks for a range of prices, generally ranging from $.69 to $1.29 each. The download market is mature but may continue to further evolve so as to set prices based on the demand for the content, especially premium content not often available on CDs (such as video).

Licensing

Obtaining licenses for digital download distribution is generally a simple one-stop affair. Distribution companies enter into agreements with record labels for the right to distribute the sound recording and then pay the record labels a license or "wholesale" fee to cover both the sound recording and the composition (mechanical) license. Record labels then pay the mechanical license to the musical composition rights owner, most often via Harry Fox.

THE WORD "LICENSE"

Question: Natalie works in the label relations department of a large company with a digital music service division. She has noticed that in some of the company's content license agreements with record labels, the labels insist on deleting the word "license" from throughout the agreement and replacing it with "distribution" or "permission" or some other similar term. Why do they do this? It is usually the more sophisticated labels that make this change.

Answer: *Record labels do not like to refer to agreements intended to govern distributors' sale of downloads as "license" agreements (even though there is a license being granted to make and sell copies of the sound recordings), as different contractual terms apply to distribution of music in agreements between record labels and artists depending on whether the distribution is a "sale" or a "license." Historically, record labels shared any revenue from the licensing of music 50/50. This was the case because there was an assumption that the artist played an active/lead role in seeking out licensing opportunities while record labels were primarily focused on marketing, tours, and record sales. On the other hand, the agreements between record labels and artists allowed for relatively small royalties for album sales—typically an 11 or 12 percent royalty rate, but an established artist can command a royalty as high as 17 to 20 percent. As a result, if record labels enter into agreements with digital music services that license such services to distribute downloads, an artist with a traditional contract could successfully claim that they are entitled to 50 percent of attributable revenue—significantly more than the few cents they typically collect for download sales today.*

In fact, major record labels have been sued on this point. As mentioned earlier, in a case decided in March of 2009 involving Eminem and Universal Music Group, a federal jury in Los Angeles sided with major labels when they denied to pay royalties on downloads of Eminem recordings at the "50

percent master license royalty" rate. However, the Ninth Circuit Court of
Appeals reversed the lower court's decision in 2010, holding that the lower
court's failure to issue a summary judgment in favor of Eminem's team was
improper and blatantly against the language of the contract.

The producers of some early Eminem recordings and the producers'
manager all had an interest in royalty payments on some of Eminem's early
recordings, and had sued UMG. At trial, UMG used Amazon as an example,
and drew a correlation between the company as a retailer of both CDs
and digital downloads to convince the jurors that the sale of both products
provided the same end result for the consumer — ownership of a copy of
an Eminem recording. The jury ultimately found that permanent downloads
are "records sold through normal retail channels," and thus royalties should
be paid to Eminem and the producers based on the much lower rate. The
appeals court found that the jury should have never heard the case, and
ultimately the case settled in 2012 before a new trial could occur in 2013.

ARE DOWNLOADS PERFORMANCES?

ASCAP has attempted in court to have a public performance royalty attributed
to a permanent download (as exists in some European territories), due to the
statutory construction of copyright law and the definition of "public performance"
including "transmissions." However, ASCAP has been unsuccessful with its
efforts. In a court decision in 2007, ASCAP lost, and ASCAP appealed to the
Second Circuit Court of Appeals, where they lost yet again, with the court stating:

> The downloads at issue in this appeal are not musical
> performances that are contemporaneously perceived by
> the listener. They are simply transfers of electronic
> files containing digital copies from an online server
> to a local hard drive. The downloaded songs are
> not performed in any perceptible manner during the
> transfers; the user must take some further action to
> play the songs after they are downloaded. Because the
> electronic download itself involves no recitation,
> rendering, or playing of the musical work encoded in
> the digital transmission, we hold that such a download
> is not a performance of that work, as defined by § 101.

—*United States v. American Society of Composers, Authors and Publishers
(ASCAP) et al.*, No. 09-0539, 2010 WL 3749292 (2nd Cir. 2010)

ASCAP appealed the U.S. Supreme Court, which declined to hear the case in
2011.

While selling permanent downloads is definitely the simplest way to distribute music online, simplicity does not necessarily mean profit. As a general rule, the margins on download sales are typically quite small (around 30 percent), and the business model is quickly being overtaken by streaming services. As demonstrated by Apple with the iPod/iTunes model, download sales are best supported if offered in conjunction with an attractive hardware offering or as an add-on to other digital music offerings such as subscription or radio services.

ON-DEMAND STREAMS

Functionality

On-demand streams provide access to music at any time; however, a connection to the Internet is required for transmission. Some services are ad-supported, but then have a premium tier offering. Premium tier access ends concurrently with one's subscription. There is no day-limited "rental" or access period.

Business Model

On-demand streams are made available via a subscription offering for a monthly fee, currently anywhere from $6 to $20, depending on the service. In recent years, however, on-demand streams are increasingly offered for free to the user and funded (from a royalty standpoint) by advertising, with a hope that the users will eventually become a subscriber (so-called "freemium tiers"). YouTube is the largest online destination for music and operates as an on-demand streaming service. Other companies that have offered this service as a subscription offering include Spotify, Apple, Rhapsody, and TIDAL. Companies that have offered advertising-supported on-demand streaming services include Spotify and YouTube. In general, record labels and music publishers are paid royalties based on usage, revenues, or subscribers, with a broad range of terms attributable to each. Depending on the royalty scheme, a licensor may benefit from high usage, high revenue (subscription and advertising), or a high volume of subscribers. Artists and other rights holders are paid pursuant to the terms of the appropriate governing agreement or under the CRB rates, if applicable. As a wide generality, but not always, the service generally keeps about 30 percent of revenue. In all cases, the business model is variable, depending on the specifics of the agreements between the record label, PRO, and the digital music distributor.

SUBSCRIPTION SERVICES VS. DOWNLOADS

Question: Michael and his lawyer friend Jared were talking about acquiring music through subscription services vs. downloads. Jared prefers his music via a subscription service; Michael prefers his in downloads that he owns. Jared told Michael that he really doesn't "own" the downloaded content anyway, so he should be happy with an all-you-can-eat access service instead. Is Jared right? Doesn't Michael own the music in the downloads he's purchased?

Answer: *Jared is correct in that Michael doesn't actually own any music he has in downloads (unless he owns the sound recording and the underlying composition of such music). Even when he "buys" a download, he is not buying the music; he is "buying" a copy—a copy that comes with numerous restrictions. For example, he can't play that copy publicly without paying a PRO for the public performance. He can't make a dozen copies for his friends without permission from the record label and publisher (and likely paying fees associated with the duplications). He can't use the song as background music for a video he makes without getting a synchronization license from the music publisher. It is this comfort with "access" in the place of "ownership" that the subscription music services have been hoping for as users adopt a rental model in place of an ownership one.*

FIG. 9.2. Rhapsody

Licensing

To license an on-demand service, distributors must obtain licenses from record labels for the sound recordings, the entities handling mechanical licensing for the reproductions of the compositions (the MLC, and any voluntarily licensed compositions through other entities), and the PROs for public performance. On-demand streaming is not subject to compulsory licensing for the sound recording under the DPRSRA and does not fall under Section 114 DMCA-compliant Internet radio, which we'll discuss in a bit.

Because mechanical royalties are a percentage of service revenue, there is a key distinction between the way mechanical royalties are paid for sales of music (in hard copies or as downloads) and how they're paid for streaming services. As we already saw, for sales of music, the current rate set by the CRB is 9.1¢ per copy made/track sold, and the record label is responsible for obtaining the mechanical license and paying the royalties. However, in digital streaming, mechanical royalties are licensed by the streaming services from the MLC and/or directly with publishers (who may use a middleman like HFA), instead of to the record label who then pays the musical composition rights holder. Prior to the MMA, digital streaming services were supposed to file a Notice of Intent (NOI) with the rights holders in order to use the composition under the compulsory licensing framework. (The failure to do so prior to the MMA led to a variety of lawsuits, which were later settled out of court. These lawsuits were caused by the inability to accurately locate rights owners. The MMA now absolves DSPs from liability provided they have procured a blanket license from the MLC.)

If you are a musical composition rights holder, you should ensure that you are registered with the MLC in order to collect the mechanical royalties due.

A CRB ruling in 2008 finally set rates for mechanical royalties due in connection with on-demand streaming (even though streaming services had already been around for several years). The rates through 2017 were 10.5% of service revenue minus PRO fees, however, these rates changed in 2018 after a new CRB ruling. For standalone portable subscription services offering interactive streaming and tethered downloads through 2022, a distributor/service must pay the mechanical royalties in the amount of the greater of (i) a percentage of revenue (from which the PRO fees are first subtracted) or (ii) a percentage of the total content cost of the service (meaning all license fees, including those paid for the sound recording), again minus the PRO fees. Because these rates are under appeal at the time of writing, you can find the specific finalized rates at 37 CFR § 385.21 - Royalty rates and calculations.

WHY DID TAYLOR SWIFT TAKE HER MUSIC OFF SPOTIFY? AREN'T THE STREAMING RATES FOR ARTISTS AND WRITERS TERRIBLY LOW?

In a very public move in November of 2014, just before the release of her album *1989*, Taylor Swift pulled all of her music from Spotify and several other streaming services, citing low payments. Others, including Aloe Blacc, have questioned their total payouts as well, with Blacc stating that he received only $4,000 in publishing royalties from 168 million streams of Avicii's "Wake Me Up." Daniel Ek, CEO of Spotify, responded to Swift, saying that she and her label were on track for around $6M in payouts in 2014, and arguing that Spotify's tremendous growth only means that number will increase.

There are likely a few things at play here. First, Taylor and her record label were likely pushing sales of the album over streams. Second, streaming must be thought of as a model that pays out over time, rather than through upfront sales of a CD. Artists and writers are only paid when their songs are listened to. Also, when we hear stories of low payouts, we don't often know where the artist or writer received their monies from—in other words, which intermediaries (like labels, PROs, subpublishers, and others) took a cut before the author received his/her check.

Royalties also are not being paid properly, sometimes due to the earlier discussed lack of rights transparency about who owns what copyright. A Berklee College of Music report in 2015 found that, depending on territory, an estimated 20–50 percent of royalties were not making it to the rightful owners, and a number of lawsuits are pending about this very issue.[1] Transparency continues to be a watchword, although various rights management services, as well as labels and publishers, in addition to the MMA, have been making progress in making digital royalties easier to collect, pay, and understand.

As technology, devices, and catalogs improve, streaming will likely end up as the dominant online business model (like Netflix for video) and revenue stream for all stakeholders in the recorded music industry. Either way, artists, labels, writers, and publishers should ensure that they are being properly compensated for distribution of their works via these channels. If, for example, music you wrote and/or recorded is available on a subscription site, you should be sure you're receiving mechanical royalties as listed above, as well as a master use fee for the recording.

---

1   "Fair Music: Transparency and Payment Flows in the Music Industry;" Berklee College of Music, 2015

TETHERED DOWNLOADS

Tethered downloads are also known as "conditional downloads," "limited downloads," or "to-go subscription/streaming."

Functionality

Tethered downloads are essentially time-limited downloads or "portable" streams. In 2004, Microsoft released "Janus," a digital-rights management technology that allowed for subscription content to be playable on a personal handheld player or a computer without a connection to the Internet. Technology has evolved, and most subscription services now offer the ability to cache subscription content onto their players or phones for listening in an "offline" mode when not connected to the Internet or a cellular network. Provided that the subscriber's account stays current and they are able to "sync" the device at least once every thirty days, the content functions similar to permanently downloaded content. Content is playable for thirty days after each sync, so failure to sync or maintain a subscription will result in disabling of the content on the player or hard drive.

IS IT POSSIBLE TO REMOVE CONTENT FROM THE MARKET?

Question: An old band of mine recorded our first album ten years ago. We then broke up and "re-banded" into our current group. Somehow, the original album is available on Spotify and TIDAL, and we don't want it to be publicly available. (The music isn't good, and it is confusing our current growing fan base.) How do we get it removed from these online sources? Can we get money from sales to date? What about Internet radio? Can we get it removed from those channels as well?

Answer: *If you are the copyright owner of the sound recording or the composition, you can use the DMCA takedown provisions set forth in Appendix F to have the content removed from these legitimate online stores. You may also pursue past royalties via such procedures by contacting the licensing department of the distributor (that may refer you to the original licensing entity). The Internet radio question is a little more complicated because Internet radio is governed by the compulsory license set forth in Section 114 of the Copyright Act. Consequently, you, the copyright owner, do not need to actually grant permission for the sound recording to be played; the right to do so is essentially required. There are certain ways to attempt to get around this, such as approaching the various Internet radio sites one by one, but it will be much harder to achieve this removal than what can be expected with a voluntary license (downloads and on-demand streams). An additional and likely more attractive option is to register with SoundExchange and collect royalties from them for the performance of your sound recordings.*

Business Model

Tethered downloads are made available via a premium subscription offering. Users pay anywhere from $10 to $20 per month for "unlimited" access to a company's catalog. Companies that have offered this service include Spotify, TIDAL, Napster, Microsoft, Rhapsody (RealNetworks), and Yahoo! Music.

As with on-demand streams, the business model varies, depending on the specifics of the agreements between the record label and the digital music distributor.

Licensing

The licensing scheme for tethered downloads can get quite complicated. Unlike the "one-stop shop" approach available for distribution of digital downloads, a digital distributor handling clearances for distribution of tethered downloads must typically obtain two licenses: one from the record label for the distribution of the sound recording, and one from the music publisher for the limited reproduction of the composition. Rates for tethered downloads are listed under "on-demand" streaming.

INTERNET RADIO

Functionality

Internet radio functions in a manner similar to on-demand streaming without the "on-demand" part. A listener can select a station, typically based on genre, and listen to streaming music for hours and hours on end. Many services, such as Pandora, offer the ability to create a station based on the listener's taste in music or selection of artists. What is different, however, is the amount of control a listener has over the content. Under the Digital Millennium Copyright Act, to qualify as a webcaster (provider of DMCA-compliant Internet radio), for the statutory DMCA rate, a rate that is significantly lower than the rates for on-demand streaming, a listener cannot skip more than a defined number of tracks in a period, display the identity of the tracks in the upcoming queue, play more than a defined number of tracks from a single artist/album within a defined period, and comply with other restrictions.

HOW TO SET UP AN INTERNET RADIO STATION

Question: What do I need to do to deliver DMCA-compliant Internet radio?

Answer: *You must comply with the eligibility requirements for a statutory license to publicly perform sound recordings, as follows:*

1. **Sound Recording Performance Complement.** "DMCA-compliant radio stations" must not exceed the "sound recording performance complement." This means that in any three-hour period, the transmitting entity may play:

   - no more than three songs from any particular album, or more than two such songs consecutively, and

   - no more than four songs by any particular recording artist, boxed set, or compilation of sound recordings (and no more than three such songs may be transmitted consecutively).

2. **Non-Interactive.** The service must be non-interactive—i.e., a user cannot receive a transmission of a program specially created for them or receive a transmission of a particular sound recording selected by them or on their behalf. (The ability of individuals to request that particular sound recordings be performed for reception by the public at large, or in the case of a subscription service, by all subscribers of the service, does not make a service interactive, if the programming on each channel of the service does not substantially consist of sound recordings that are performed within one hour of the request or at a time designated by either the transmitting entity or the individual making such request.)

3. **Prior Announcements.** The transmitting entity may not publish program schedules in advance or make prior announcements of the titles of specific songs, albums, or recording artists featured on the program. However, a transmitting entity may announce that a particular recording artist will be included within an unspecified future time period. The transmitting entity may identify the specific sound recording immediately before it is performed and may name artists as illustrative examples of the kinds of artists generally played on a particular program or station.

4. **Textual Data.** The transmission of each song must be accompanied by text identifying the title of the sound recording, the name of the phonorecord on which it can be found, and the name of the featured artist, if any.

5. **Repeat Programming.** Looped or continuous predetermined programs must be at least three hours long. Archived programs (available for Web users to hear on demand) must be at least five hours long and even then must be available to the end user for no more than two weeks. Regularly scheduled rebroadcasts of predetermined programs are permitted to occur in a two-week period only three times if less than an hour in length and only four times if an hour or more in length.

6. **Images.** The service must not transmit images contemporaneously with sound recordings in a manner that suggests an affiliation or association between the sound recording copyright owner or featured artist and a particular product or service advertised by the transmitting entity.

7. **Piracy Concerns.** The transmitting entity may not cause or induce the making of a digital copy of the content, and must use technology reasonably available to it to limit the recipient from making digital copies. Further, the transmitting entity must cooperate in order to prevent any person or entity from automatically scanning the entity's transmissions in order to select a particular sound recording. Finally, the transmitting entity may not remove any DRM technology that was placed in a file by the sound recording copyright owner and must ensure such anti-theft features are not removed during the transmission process.

8. **Already Released to Public.** The transmitting entity may not transmit any sound recording that has not already been released for broadcast or sale to the public under authority of the copyright owner unless it receives permission from the copyright owner to do so.

9. **No Channel Switching.** The transmitting entity may not cause any device receiving the transmission to switch from one program channel to another.

Business Model

Like on-demand streaming, Internet radio is generally made available as a subscription or advertising-supported offering. Subscriptions run on average $5 per month while advertising-supported models are free to the end user. In general, due to the historically low royalty rates for Internet radio, the margins on Internet radio subscription products are generally better for distributors but less profitable for rights holders.

Licensing

In the 1990s, the DPRSRA established a "statutory" or "compulsory" license to stream sound recordings as long as the music being streamed complies with applicable restrictions. This means that services need not obtain direct licenses from each sound recording copyright owner provided that they comply with the rules and pay the appropriate royalty. Sound recording royalties are paid to SoundExchange, an entity that was previously a division of the RIAA but now operates as a stand-alone non-profit for this purpose (see chapter 3). Publishing royalties are paid to PROs.

New royalty rates for the public performance of the sound recording were set in June of 2021. (See the "Royalties on Webcasts" sidebar in chapter 3.)

Some services which offer a "radio" option in addition to on-demand streaming may also choose to "go-direct" with the licensing of their radio offering, including the radio option as part of their negotiated license with the record label for their on-demand streams. This gives the services greater programming flexibility on the radio offering and avoidance of adherence to Section 114 rate restrictions.

AD-SUPPORTED

Though not a delivery format, per se, it is worth noting that any and all of the above offerings can also be made available to end users for free, legally, provided that the distributor still licenses the music and pays proper royalties to the rights holders. This can be done via an advertising-supported offering where the distributor uses the revenue from advertisements to pay the costs of license fees and running the service.

Numerous ad-supported services have been offered in the last five years; few have been particularly successful. Even YouTube is not particularly profitable. That said, the business model appears to continue to attract attention, with new services entering the market at least monthly. *For artists, this means that you will need to ensure that any agreements with publishing companies, record labels, or other middlemen between your work and your fans include provisions regarding royalties collected from advertising sales in addition to straight sales or subscription revenue.*

ROYALTY-RATE-SETTING EXAMPLE: PANDORA MEDIA, INC. V. AMERICAN SOCIETY OF COMPOSERS, AUTHORS, AND PUBLISHERS (ASCAP)

In a case between Pandora and ASCAP, brought by Pandora to rate court in the Southern District of New York under ASCAP's consent decree, Pandora sought to establish its royalty rate for ASCAP repertoire through the end of 2015. Pandora argued that the rates it had been paying (1.85 percent of service revenue) to ASCAP were too high and that the company was not profitable, requesting a rate of 1.7 percent instead. ASCAP in turn argued that Pandora wasn't paying enough, and should be paying as high as 3 percent of its revenue in future years, with testimony stating that Pandora in 2012 paid $200M to record labels for the right to use sound recordings, but only $20M to writers and publishers for musical works.

As we discussed earlier, publishers had attempted to withdraw their new media rights from the PROs so they could negotiate directly with the digital services, and had actually come to agreement with some major services before the court's separate decision that publishers cannot selectively place rights with ASCAP and BMI. The dispute was finally settled in late 2015 when Pandora signed new licensing agreements with both ASCAP and BMI, the terms of which were not made public (since they were not set by the rate court).

FREE/PROMOTIONAL/UPSELL OFFERINGS

Similar to the need to carefully monitor potential revenues from advertising supported products, artists and other creators need to be increasingly diligent about ensuring they are properly licensing and collecting appropriate royalties from promotional or free offerings—offerings that are typically associated with enticing users to buy more from or subscribe to a service. For example, are you being paid when your music is being streamed in thirty-second preview clips on iTunes?

ROYALTIES ON MARKETING FREEBIES

Question: I am a country artist. I write and perform my own music. My record label, the same label I have been with for fifteen years, pays me for download sales with iTunes, Amazon, and others, but I don't ever receive payments for distribution via "free" advertising-supported and subscription services, though I know my most recent albums are on at least a few of them. Where is this money going? Am I due a portion of that revenue? I know that my record label has a deal with at least two subscription services.

Answer: *It depends. If your contract with your record label specifies that you are due royalties for digital distribution of your music beyond track sales, you should be getting paid. If not, the label is rightfully keeping that revenue to itself. The best thing to do at this point is to review your contract, perhaps with the assistance of a music attorney, and determine what your best course of action is to start sharing in that revenue stream for the distribution of your works. Further, it is likely that you are due fees for the public performance of your works (if you own the compositions). You should work with the PROs with whom you are engaged in pursuit of these royalties.*

PAYOUTS

So, how do payouts work, from digital services? As we've seen in figure 5.2, in general, a streaming service pays a government mandated percentage of its revenue for mechanical and public performance royalties. For downloads and physical (CD/vinyl) purchase, the rate remains a "penny-rate" of 9.1 cents per reproduction made (vinyl pressed, or downloads sold, since the reproduction of a download happens at sale.)

Services keep about 30 percent of the money that comes in for overhead (the exception is YouTube, which keeps about 50 percent and argues that the costs of its ad sales warrant additional fees), which leaves about 60 percent for record labels. (A 2014 study by the French trade group SNEP found that labels keep about 73 percent of all monies paid to rights holders, after artists are paid their royalties and musical compositions rights holders collect their share.[2])

2　www.musicbusinessworldwide.com/artists-get-7-of-streaming-cash-labels-take-46/

Why is the sound recording so valuable? It depends on who you ask. Labels note that they spend a lot of money on recording and marketing costs, and that their recording could be re-recorded again, bringing a secondary revenue stream to the musical composition that the sound recording will never have. Publishers will argue that writers have no alternative revenue streams (i.e., they don't tour), and that they should be entitled to a larger share (some even argue the split should be 50/50) but the regulation of royalty rates for musical compositions leaves them at a disadvantage in the negotiating process. Both are logical arguments, but logic doesn't always apply in a highly fragmented industry like music! In sum, business models and distribution formats will continue to evolve. It is important for all stakeholders in the creation, licensing, and distribution chain to stay on top of this quickly evolving industry so as to ensure that they are active participants. Artists need to be on top of their agreements. Other licensors (labels, publishers) need to closely monitor their licensees, and licensees need to be proactive in the marketplace for their business to thrive.

TRANSPARENCY IN THE DIGITAL MUSIC INDUSTRY: SONY -W- SPOTIFY

Frustrated by low payouts, artists and writers and their representatives continue their calls for greater transparency in the streaming music industry, demanding faster, better data from their labels and publishers about their streaming earnings. (Savvy artist managers have also recognized that geographical streaming data can be key for tour development and routing, since they can see where an artist is popular, potentially in real-time, from streaming.)

Confusion has also ensued about how payments come from the services to rights owners, and standard contractual confidentiality clauses have kept the deal points a secret, for the most part. So when, in May 2015, someone leaked a confidential Sony Music contract with Spotify, the digital music community was greatly intrigued and spent time digging into the details. The contract provided for annual advances to be paid to the label from Spotify, immediately prompting questions from managers about whether any unearned advances (called "digital breakage") are shared with artists. (Warner showed that they had been paying breakage since 2009, while Sony immediately committed to do so.) Sony also had a most-favored nations clause in the agreement, preventing other labels from getting a better deal, and Spotify was able to keep up to 15 percent of revenues from ad sales made by third parties. Finally, the per-stream payout section showed a hugely complex, multi-page formula with both revenue sharing and a per-subscriber minimum payout in the event that it exceeds the revenue sharing amount. The question of "how much does Spotify pay per stream" wasn't resolved by the contract—because there is no consistent "per-stream" rate, and the rate varies from month to month based on usage and subscriber numbers.

So, How Do Streaming Services Calculate Their Revenue to Be Paid?

We often hear that streaming services pay out rights owners based on a percentage of revenue and rights holders' number of streams. But what exactly does this mean? Most services create a total revenue pool and a total number of streams, usually per territory and pay licensors based their pro-rata shares. However, much discussion continues about a program of user-centric payouts—meaning that each user's revenue is divided by that user's streams and his/her subscription fees only go to those artist to whom he/she has listened. It is often thought that such a system would benefit more middle and long tail artists, who lose when all user revenue goes into a total pool. Many users may only listen to ten songs (or one hundred or one thousand) from niche artists in a month, but in the larger pool of streams, the artist wouldn't see as much revenue because the top artists have such incredible numbers of streams in a larger pool. As of writing, Deezer and SoundCloud are experimenting with a user-centric payout system.

CHAPTER 10

CRB Rate Decisions and Royalty Payments

WHAT IS THE CRB?

We've mentioned the Copyright Royalty Board, or CRB, quite a bit so far. This enigmatic body is a panel of three judges appointed by the Librarian of Congress under the Copyright Royalty and Distribution Reform Act of 2004. The judges sit for six-year staggered terms, and are responsible for making most regulated royalty setting decisions in the U.S. (except with ASCAP and BMI, which are set by rate court decisions under their consent decrees). Judges must have been practicing lawyers for at least seven years. One judge is named as the Chief Copyright Royalty Judge, while one of the other two must have substantive experience in law and the other substan-tive experience in economics. The judges hear cases related to mechanical royalties, streaming, and satellite radio, among others. They must set royalty rates based on some over-arching objectives already discussed on page 48.

WHO ARE THE TYPICAL PARTIES IN A CRB HEARING?

So, who typically gets involved when it's time to set rates? In recent hearings for royalties from digital services, the major parties are usually the lobbying groups: National Music Publishers' Association (NMPA), the Recording Industry Association of America (RIAA), and the Digital Media Association (DiMA), which represents some of the digital services. Specific parties may get involved as well if the hearing results will directly impact their business, such as SiriusXM, ASCAP or BMI, labels, publishers, or Pandora. (This list is by no means exhaustive; any party who will be directly impacted by royalty rate setting can participate.)

MECHANICAL ROYALTY RATE SETTING UNDER SECTION 115

One of the most important tasks undertaken by the CRB is the review of mechanical royalty rates. As discussed earlier, publishing rates are highly regulated in the U.S., with mechanical licenses compulsory for any previously released musical works with rates set by the CRB.

Development of the online music marketplace led to a lot of frustration about what type of music delivery was what type of product. In 2001, the RIAA asked the Copyright Office to enumerate specifically what types of deliveries were considered "digital phonorecord deliveries (DPDs)." Several questions were raised. For example, are "incidental DPDs" through a stream covered by the compulsory license? What is the royalty rate for streams?

Licensing of mechanical royalties for digital music services became a bit clearer under a settlement reached by the NMPA, RIAA, and the Harry Fox Agency (HFA) in 2001, which allowed for bulk licensing of all reproduction rights needed for digital music services, including server copies, buffer copies, streams, and tethered downloads. The RIAA had applied Section 115 of the copyright code that allows for the "rental" of a phonorecord if a royalty is paid.

Under the agreement, RIAA members (labels) who wished to license to digital music services could procure the mechanical licenses from HFA, then subsequently license the works as a whole to a digital music service. The first service to avail itself of the new option was Rhapsody, then the digital music arm of Listen.com.

The agreement was set out while the parties waited for the Copyright Arbitration Royalty Panel (the predecessor to the CRB) to set royalty rates for digital services. Under the agreement, RIAA paid an immediate advance of $1,000,000 to HFA and $62,500/month until the royalty rates were set. This continued until 2008, when the CRB finally issued their rulings. (We'll discuss those later in this chapter.)

2009 SETTLEMENT

In 2006, the CRB announced that it would be undertaking proceedings to determine which licenses and royalties applied to which
digital deliveries. An initial negotiation period between the parties
was unsuccessful, and multiple Congressional and CRB hearings were
held in 2007 and 2008. Congress failed to elucidate whether it expected
certain provisions of the Copyright Act to apply to certain deliveries,
leaving the CRB in a tenuous position. The Copyright Office was forced
to open a rulemaking proceeding to interpret the Copyright Act, and
in late 2008 issued an interim rule allowing services who deliver DPDs
to be covered for all licenses needed (e.g., server copies, etc.) by one
reproduction license.

Meanwhile, in the spring of 2008, the NMPA, RIAA, and DiMA
announced that they had reached an agreement on rates for streaming
and tethered downloads, which was accepted by the court and adopted
(see chapter 9).

2012 SETTLEMENT

Another settlement occurred in 2012, with the CRB continuing the 2008
royalty rates for the previously agreed uses, but adding rates for five
new categories of works:

1. **Mixed service bundles** (a locker service, limited interactive
   service, downloads or ringtones combined with a non-music
   product, e.g., a mobile phone, consumer electronics device, or
   Internet service) for 11.35 percent of revenue or 21 percent of
   total content cost, whichever is greater.

2. **Paid locker services** (subscription-based locker, e.g., iTunes,
   providing on-demand streaming and downloads) for 12 percent
   of revenue or 20.65 percent of total content cost or 17 cents per
   subscriber, whichever is greater.

3. **Purchased content locker services** (a free digital locker that
   provides free "cloud storage" to a purchaser of a permanent
   digital download, ringtone, or CD) for 12 percent of revenue or
   22 percent of total content cost, whichever is greater.

4. **"Limited offerings"** (e.g., limited interactive subscription-based service offering limited genres of music or specialized playlists) for 10.5 percent of revenue or 21 percent of total content cost or 18 cents per subscriber, whichever is greater.

5. **Music bundles** (e.g., CD with download, ringtones, and permanent digital downloads) for 11.35 percent of revenue or 21 percent of total content cost.

WEBCASTING ROYALTY RATE SETTING

Webcasting royalty rates for the public performance of sound recordings under DMCA compliant non-interactive stations as we discussed previously in chapter 3, to be paid under DPRSRA to Sound Exchange, are also set by the CRB under Section 114. It is incredibly complicated, with different rates depending on the size of the broadcaster, whether they operate commercially or non-commercially, and whether or not they have a subscription offering. For now, you probably only need to know that the rates for commercial broadcasters are set per-performance rates (i.e., the rates for performing one sound recording to one listener). The 2021–2025 rates are $.0021 per performance (the rate paid per song per listener) rate for non-subscription streaming, and $.0026 per performance for subscription streaming.

PANDORA BOUGHT AN FM RADIO STATION IN AN ATTEMPT TO LOWER ITS RATES

In 2013, Pandora purchased KXMZ, a small Rapid City, South Dakota radio station. Did Pandora plan to enter the terrestrial radio business? No. Instead they hoped to take advantage of lower rates paid to ASCAP and BMI by streaming stations that are owned by terrestrial radio stations. In 2014, the FCC denied the takeover by Pandora of the radio license because Pandora had not sufficiently demonstrated its domestic and foreign ownership percentages were compliant with the FCC rules. Did it work out for Pandora? No, but it's another great example of companies getting creative about lowering or increasing their royalty structures, depending on which side of the fence they sit.

2016 SETTLEMENT

Under the terms of a settlement reached by the NMPA and its members with Spotify in early 2016, in response to some of the many lawsuits about unpaid mechanical royalties from digital services, Spotify paid $30 million to the NMPA. The sum of $25M of the funds was to be disbursed to NMPA members based claims, with any unclaimed money paid out on market share. (This is a typical payout process, often called the "black box"; when a service doesn't know who to pay, the unpaid royalties are usually paid out based on industry market share, which seems to benefit major labels and publishers, especially given that the unpaid monies are more likely than not owed to small publishers and individual writers who did not know how to collect them.) An additional $5M was dedicated directly to payments by market share to the publishers.

CHAPTER 11

Gaps in Copyright Law

Intellectual property law suffers, perhaps more than any other substantive area of law, from an inability to keep up with innovation. As technologies continue to develop and enter the marketplace at an exponential rate, current laws and guidelines struggle to keep up and protect rights holders while encouraging innovation. Copyright law is no exception.

Initially created to govern the making of physical copies of an author's works, copyright law has been particularly challenged by the Internet and the ease of copying and distribution that it allows (and in some cases, encourages). With books, music, film, software, images, videos, and numerous other forms of authored works easily duplicated and widely disseminated—often anonymously, with a press of a button—it is an uphill and arguably losing battle for rights holders to try to control or monitor.

We saw this play out in a particularly painful way in the music industry. Several years ago, according to the International Federation of the Phonographic Industry (IFPI), the music industry was half the size it was in 2000, prior to the development of Napster. However, in recent years the emergence and consumer uptake of access-based music subscription services has reinvigorated the music market. Companies are making substantial investments in the space, and artists and writers are beginning to see the fruits of the turnaround. If subscription continues to grow worldwide, the music industry will be substantially larger in coming years than its prior peak in 2000.

Congress has tried to anticipate future delivery schemes for music and other copyrighted works, with amendments such as the Digital Millennium Copyright Act, and updates to copyright law are commonly considered as a response to a specific technology, as seen earlier in the case of the DAT and the Audio Home Recording Act. Legislation was also introduced to address one of the first websites to serve music consumers, MP3.com, which allowed consumers to listen to copies of music that they already own from any computer connected to the Internet. Consumers merely needed to verify their ownership of a CD by inserting the CD into their computer and allowing the site to authenticate its presence. The site was eventually shut down, but it is important to any study of attempts to change the laws for the digital distribution of music online because legislation was offered specifically to make the MP3 .com service legal. Amy Harmon noted in the *New York Times* that:

> *The proposed legislation is written so narrowly that it almost seems tailored to serve the specific interests of MP3.com. And no one thinks that it will pass before Congress recesses. But the bill is significant because, for the first time in this year's digital music wars, it raises the question of what is right rather than what is legal.... The company's star lawyer, David Boies, who successfully argued the Justice Department's antitrust case against Microsoft last year, has lots of arguments why Napster is blameless. What if he's right? What if existing copyright law did not envision the ability to copy on the mass scale made possible by the Internet? Does that mean that such copying should be allowed, or should the law be modified? But at a time when technology is evolving so rapidly and the stakes are so high over who can exercise how much control over copyrighted works, there may be cause for Congress to look more closely at the rights it has doled out in the past, and how those rights are being applied now.*[1]

Harmon raises a valid point. With mega-corporations controlling copyrighted works for ever-increasing copyright durations, does it make sense to continue restricting rights? On the flip side, does it spur creativity to have creative works floating around for free? These are some examples of the weighty questions that must be asked every time a change to the law is contemplated. The political climate in Washington has made change difficult, but as seen with the MMA, passed unanimously, parties can occasionally agree on a solution.

---

1   Harmon, Amy. "New Economy: With music widely available online, is it now time to tighten copyright laws or consider rewriting them to reflect reality?" *The New York Times*. 2 October, 2000.

PRE-1972 SOUND RECORDINGS

One anomaly in copyright law recently solved by the passage of the MMA was the lack of federal copyright protection for sound recordings created prior to 1972, when the law was changed to allow U.S. copyright to include sound recordings. Given that Aretha Franklin, Marvin Gaye, the Beatles, and other high profile acts recorded some of their most popular works in the 1960's, these songs were not eligible for the benefit of the DPRSRA and had to rely on state copyright law if they wanted protection. The MMA resolved the issue: it did not retroactively give full copyright protection to these recordings, but did provide a mechanism for their owners to now collect royalties for their use as digital transmissions (Pandora, Spotify, etc.). Prior to the change, the group the Turtles had filed and won a lawsuit against SiriusXM under California state copyright for performing their sound recordings without a license.

SIGNIFICANT LITIGATION

A&M Records et al. v. Napster, decided by the Ninth Circuit Court of Appeals in 2001, is probably the most recognizable case to be decided on copyright and digital distribution of music to date. The ruling essentially shut down Napster in its former incarnation and set the stage for future law-driven clampdowns on P2P distribution of media online.

As discussed, Napster was the world's first large scale peer-to-peer file sharing service, meaning that the service enabled users to search the hard drives of other users connected to the service, and connect with one another to share files. Sued by A&M and other record labels assisted by the RIAA, Napster argued in court that since they were not actually providing the copyrighted files, but rather just enabling communication, the company could not be held liable for copyright infringement under the "service provider" exception of the DMCA, discussed in chapter 12. Napster also presented the defense of fair use, based on the theories that the service also enabled the sharing of authorized music from new artists, sampling, and "space-shifting," a variation of defense used by Sony in the landmark Betamax case in the 1980s.

Napster lost in district court, where Judge Marilyn Patel stated that:

Although downloading and uploading MP3 music files is not paradigmatic commercial activity, it is also not personal use in the traditional sense. Plaintiffs have not shown that the majority of Napster users download music to sell—that is, for profit. However, given the vast scale of Napster use among anonymous individuals, the court finds that downloading and uploading MP3 music files with the assistance of Napster are not private uses. At the very least, a host user sending a file cannot be said to engage in a personal use when distributing that file to an anonymous requester. Moreover, the fact that Napster users get for free something they would ordinarily have to buy suggests that they reap economic advantages from Napster use.[2]

Napster appealed the decision to the Ninth Circuit Court of Appeals, where they lost yet again, resulting in an injunction requiring Napster to remove all copyrighted material from the service. The injunction led to the shutdown of the Napster service because the company did not have the technology to filter files and comply with the injunction. At the time, Napster had a verified user base of over 25 million people.

A&M RECORDS, INC. V. NAPSTER, 239 F.3D 1004, (9TH CIR. 2001)

Numerous guiding principles were derived from the Ninth Circuit opinion, including the following three particularly relevant guidelines:

1. The free, unlicensed downloading of a complete audio file as a "sample" does not qualify for a fair use defense.

   The record supports a finding that free promotional downloads are highly regulated by the record company plaintiffs and that the companies collect royalties for song samples available on retail Internet sites. The district court further found that both the market for audio CDs and market for online distribution are adversely affected by Napster's service. The court did not abuse its discretion when it found that, overall, Napster has an adverse impact on the audio CD and digital download markets. The record supports the district court's preliminary determinations that: (1) the more music that sampling users download, the less likely they are to eventually purchase the recordings on audio CD; and (2) even if the audio CD market is not harmed, Napster has adverse effects on the developing digital download market.[3]

2   *A&M Records, Inc. v. Napster, Inc.*, 114 F. Supp. 2d 896 (N.D. Cal. 2000).
3   *A&M Records, Inc. v. Napster*, 239 F.3d 1004, (9th Cir. 2001)

2. Napster's space-shifting is not fair use. Space-shifting—the practice of downloading an MP3 file of a track already owned on a CD for listening elsewhere—was yet another feature of the Napster service that was deemed not eligible for a fair use defense, a defense that had been successfully applied to other contexts (such as VHS videotapes).

   It is obvious that once a user lists a copy of music he already owns on the Napster system in order to access the music from another location, the song becomes "available to millions of other individuals," not just the original CD owner. [4]

3. A distributor can be held to be a "vicarious infringer" for failure to control or stop infringing activities when they are financially benefiting and have the ability to supervise, but do not do so. Because Napster failed to actively police their users, the company could be held liable for vicarious infringement.

   In the context of copyright law, vicarious liability extends beyond an employer/employee relationship to cases in which a defendant "has the right and ability to supervise the infringing activity and also has a direct financial interest in such activities. . . Financial benefit exists where the availability of infringing material "acts as a 'draw' for customers . . . Napster's future revenue is directly dependent upon 'increases in userbase.'" Here, plaintiffs have demonstrated that Napster retains the right to control access to its system. Napster has an express reservation of rights policy, stating on its website that it expressly reserves the "right to refuse service and terminate accounts in [its] discretion, including, but not limited to, if Napster believes that user conduct violates applicable law, or for any reason in Napster's sole discretion, with or without cause." To escape imposition of vicarious liability, the reserved right to police must be exercised to its fullest extent. Turning a blind eye to detectable acts of infringement for the sake of profit gives rise to liability. [5]

   See appendix C for a longer excerpt of this case.

---

4   *A&M Records, Inc. v. Napster,* 239 F.3d 1004, (9th Cir. 2001)
5   Ibid.

METRO-GOLDWYN-MAYER STUDIOS INC., ET AL. V. GROKSTER, LTD., 545 U.S. 913 (2005)

Four years after Napster, in yet another very notable ruling on copyright and music law, the U.S. Supreme Court in 2005 heard the case of *Metro-Goldwyn-Mayer Studios Inc., et al. v. Grokster, Ltd.* (Note that the Napster case went only to U.S. Court of Appeals for the Ninth Circuit, and was not decided by the Supreme Court.)

The facts leading up to the case were quite simple. The defendants (Grokster and StreamCast) distributed free software products that allowed computer users to share electronic files through P2P networks. The Grokster and StreamCast (Morpheus) products were slightly different from the original Napster, in that their products merely enabled users to search the computers of other users. The products were cleverly designed so that at no point was the search communication processed by any of the defendants' products.

Recognizing the similarity in use and functionality, a collective of copyright holders (MGM, with other motion picture studios, recording companies, songwriters, and music publishers) sued Grokster and StreamCast for their users' copyright infringements. Their claim was that the defendants knowingly and intentionally distributed their software products to enable users to reproduce and distribute copyrighted works in violation of basic copyright law.

The question addressed by the Court was "under what circumstances the distributor of a product capable of both lawful and unlawful use is liable for the acts of copyright infringement by third parties using the product." The Court held that those who distribute and promote an object that fosters infringement can be held liable for the infringing acts of its users (third parties):

> *...that one who distributes a device with the object of promoting its use to infringe copyright, as shown by clear expression or other affirmative steps taken to foster infringement, is liable for the resulting acts of infringement by third parties.*[6]

---

6   *Metro-Goldwyn-Mayer Studios Inc., Et Al. v. Grokster, Ltd.*, 545 U.S. 913 (2005)

The case is of interest for numerous reasons. For one, the intent behind the development of a music distribution product and whether its users' actions are monitored can define whether it is a legal one. As stated by the Court:

> *Grokster and StreamCast are not, however, merely passive recipients of information about infringing use. The record is replete with evidence that from the moment Grokster and StreamCast began to distribute their free software, each one clearly voiced the objective that recipients use it to download copyrighted works, and each took active steps to encourage infringement.* [7]

Evidence had been introduced at trial showing that the companies actively promoted the illegal uses of their product. Further:

> *Finally, there is no evidence that either company made an effort to filter copyrighted material from users' downloads or otherwise impede the sharing of copyrighted files. Although Grokster appears to have sent emails warning users about infringing content when it received threatening notice from the copyright holders, it never blocked anyone from continuing to use its software to share copyrighted files. StreamCast not only rejected another company's offer of help to monitor infringement, but blocked the Internet Protocol addresses of entities it believed were trying to engage in such monitoring on its networks...* [8]

Summing up their decision, the Court stated:

> *[O]ne who distributes a device with the object of promoting its use to infringe copyright, as shown by clear expression or other affirmative steps taken to foster infringement, is liable for the resulting acts of infringement by third parties.* [9]

And with that, the Supreme Court of the United States attempted to further control the availability of products that can be (and are primarily used) for infringing purposes.

See appendix D for a longer excerpt of this case.

---

7   *Metro-Goldwyn-Mayer Studios Inc., Et Al. v. Grokster, Ltd.*, 545 U.S. 913 (2005)
8   Ibid.
9   Ibid.

VIACOM INTERNATIONAL INC. V. YOUTUBE, INC.

In a case brought by Viacom against YouTube in 2007, Viacom contended that the defendants had induced infringement and deliberately built a business on third party copyrighted content. YouTube moved for dismissal via summary judgment, which was granted in 2010 on the grounds that YouTube had complied with all relevant provisions of the DMCA safe harbor, thus shielding themselves from liability, and that YouTube had no duty to analyze each and every video uploaded to their site, as doing so would controvert the intentions of the DMCA. Viacom appealed to the Second Circuit Court of Appeals, and the summary judgment was partially overturned and the case remanded to the lower court, with the lower court judge again granting summary judgment for YouTube in 2013.

The district court judge based his ruling on four factors, which were sent down to him from the appeals court:

> *Whether ... YouTube had knowledge or awareness of any specific infringements ... ; (B) Whether ... YouTube willfully blinded itself ...; (C) Whether YouTube had the "right and ability to control" infringing activity ...; and (D) Whether any clips ... were syndicated ...* [10]

Despite evidence that YouTube had decided not to police content unless owners had licensed the material to YouTube, the judge found that YouTube had no duty to police the infringement, as long as they complied with the safe harbor, stating that:

> *Knowledge of the prevalence of infringing activity, and welcoming it, does not itself forfeit the safe harbor. To forfeit that, the provider must influence or participate in the infringement.* [11]

The parties eventually settled the case out of court in 2014.

---

10 *Viacom v. YouTube*, 2d Cir. April 5, 2012
11 Ibid.

LACK OF COPYRIGHT REGISTRIES

Another major gap for decades in U.S. copyright law was the lack of a central clearinghouse for music rights. Even though copyright has required a work to be "identified" with the copyright office in order to receive royalties under a compulsory mechanical license, the process has been complicated, opaque, and difficult for streaming services. The passage of the MMA and creation of the MLC were meant to resolve this issue, providing a mechanism for a blanket license. Services and rights owners can still enter into voluntary direct licenses, which would remove those directly licensed works from the blanket license granted by the MLC. It remains to be seen how the operation of the MLC will evolve in its first few years of operation.

CHAPTER 12

DMCA/Copyright Law Reform

The Digital Millennium Copyright Act ("DMCA") was signed into law by Bill Clinton in 1998. Among other things, the DMCA served two primary purposes: (1) to extend the reach of copyright law in the digital age, and (2) to limit the liability of the providers of online services for copyright infringement by their users. The law, meant to bring U.S. law into compliance with the World Intellectual Property Organization ("WIPO") treaties, criminalized the production and dissemination of technology, devices, or services intended to circumvent measures that control access to copyrighted works (e.g., DRM), as well as the act of actually circumventing an access control, such as tampering with a digital fingerprint. The law makes such activities criminal whether or not there is actual infringement of copyright itself.

To limit liability of service providers, the DMCA sets forth certain guidelines that if followed, relieve such providers of legal exposure and risk associated with their otherwise innocent delivery of infringing works.

For example, the DMCA provides a "safe harbor" for ISPs (a limitation on liability for infringement), stating that service providers who merely provide a gateway to the Internet (e.g., AT&T or Comcast) cannot be held liable for the infringing acts of their customers/users. However, the limited liability of ISPs exists only in cases where the ISP meets certain conditions including giving the infringing end-users warnings that what they are doing is wrong and terminating repeat offenders. (It was this safe harbor provision that the original Napster tried to hide behind in its 2000 to 2001 battle with record labels, which we addressed in chapter 8.)

ISPs, however, have been working with the music industry to cut piracy under the DMCA, sometimes involuntarily. As part of its enforcement efforts against piracy, the RIAA in 2003 began filing civil lawsuits against individuals who illegally traded music online. In order to identify such users, the RIAA needed data from ISPs, and served the service providers with subpoenas under the DMCA demanding the identity of users tied to Internet Protocol (IP) addresses known to be used in sharing music online.

For example, the RIAA used the subpoena power in section 512(h) of the DMCA to request the identity of Verizon Internet users who were thought to be involved in piracy via P2P networks. In this case, Verizon refused to comply with the RIAA order, arguing that the Verizon network did not actually store the material but instead merely transmitted it. The court held that the RIAA was not able to use the DMCA subpeona clause to acquire the identities, but Verizon was forced to eventually turn over the names when the RIAA began filing "John Doe" lawsuits. The RIAA ultimately sued over two thousand individuals for copyright infringement. The vast majority of the cases against individual file-sharers were settled out of court.

Under the DMCA, a "safe harbor" also exists for user-generated content services such as YouTube (as seen in the Viacom case), which might actually store infringing material, if they meet the following requirements:

1. They do not receive a financial benefit directly attributable to the infringing activity.

2. They are not aware of the presence of infringing material or know any facts or circumstances that would make infringing material apparent.

3. Upon receiving notice from copyright owners or their agents, they act expeditiously to remove the purported infringing material.

The DMCA has remained the subject of great debate and in recent years, including high profile litigation, such as *Viacom v. YouTube*, which we just discussed in Chapter 10.

Separately, in *IO Group Inc. v. Veoh Networks Inc.*, a case with similar facts, the U.S. District Court for the Northern District of California ruled that the defendant Veoh qualified for protection under the safe harbor of the DMCA. Veoh had made it clear that it regarded copyright infringement as a serious matter by responding to DMCA takedown notices within twenty-four hours, registering a Copyright Agent with the Copyright Office, providing warnings to users about infringement, and terminating repeat infringers. Many believe that the law can and should be credited with the concentration of highly successful online distribution companies in the United States. Regardless of what one thinks of it, the DMCA safe harbor remains a powerful, yet highly contentious piece of legislation in the United States—a law that shapes much of online media distribution generally. (The EU also has codified a similar safe harbor provision, modeled on that of the DMCA.)

So, what does the DMCA have to do with music law? A lot. Depending on where one falls in the digital music distribution food chain from creator to consumer, the DMCA largely shapes the way music is distributed online, and why. The law also creates a standard for starting an Internet radio station, as discussed in chapter 8. We will give examples of its application to each of the primary players in the distribution chain.

THE DMCA AND THE MUSIC BUSINESS

There are numerous ways that the DMCA could come into play in the digital music industry. We will focus on three primary examples in a Q&A format: (1) an artist who finds her work available via an online music store without any knowledge of how it got there, (2) an independent record label that has licensed its catalog to an ad-supported streaming service only to find that the service won't distribute half of it "due to DMCA takedowns from a music publisher," and (3) a digital distributor that receives dozens of demands for removal of content weekly.

How Do I Use the DMCA to Remove My Content from a Website?

Question: I recorded a solo album three years ago. I sold several thousand copies on tour, via my own website (linked from my Facebook page) and other online sources. I never signed with a record label or licensed this album for any online distribution, but I am considering doing so in the future. Last week, I found this album streaming on two major online music services. What should I do to have it removed?

Answer: The DMCA will provide complete guidance on how to proceed, but the first step is to look at the distributor website's Terms of Service or Terms of Use, typically found via a link on one of the first pages of the Web store. Find the name and address of the store's designated

"Copyright Agent" and send them what is known in the industry as a "DMCA Takedown Notice" (see chapter 15 for a sample takedown notice). A takedown notice must be in writing and must include:

1. the physical or electronic signature of the one asserting the right to takedown,

2. identification of the work allegedly infringed,

3. identification of the allegedly infringing material sufficiently to permit the distributor to find, remove, and/or limit access,

4. the sender's contact information,

5. a statement that the complaining party has a good faith belief that use of the material is not authorized, and

6. a statement that the information in the notice is accurate and, under penalty of perjury, that either the owner or the complaining party is authorized to act on behalf of the owner of an exclusive right that is allegedly infringed. [1]

Once the distributor company has received a proper DMCA takedown notice that satisfies these six requirements, they must remove the content until further notice. It is then up to you to work with the distributor or the original licensor to obtain an accounting and/or reporting information about prior distribution and associated royalties, if any. Depending on the nature of the parties, this process could take some time in part because governing license agreements typically contain confidentiality commitments, indemnification provisions, and other limitations on sharing of such information.

Alternatively, you could pursue a license with the distributing entity so that instead of taking the content down, they start to pay you the royalties attributable to the distribution of the work. This can be achieved by requesting licensing information rather than a takedown. Note that this same analysis applies to on-demand streams in addition to downloads; both require a license and can be removed for lack thereof.

---

[1]   17 U.S.C. § 512(c)(3)

What about the Interplay Between Publishers and Record Labels in a DMCA World?

Question: I own a mid-size independent record label with about five hundred signed artists. We recently did a distribution deal with a popular ad-supported streaming service only to find that the service won't distribute half of our product "due to DMCA takedowns from a music publisher." What does this mean?

Answer: This means that a music publisher claiming rights in the underlying compositions to that portion of your catalog has sent a takedown notice, as we discussed above, to the service and that the service has complied. If you want the catalog reinstated on the service, your best bet is to contact the music publisher and see if you can work together to come to an agreement on acceptable license terms.

What Does the DMCA Have to Do with Sublicensing Online?

Question: I run the content operations division of a niche digital music service. Every week, we receive dozens of emails from artists, labels, heirs to artists, and others saying that they did not give us permission to make content that they own available on our service. I have had our licensing attorney check the source of the allegedly unlicensed content, and it turns out that in 99 percent of cases, the content is, in fact, licensed to us by a label or aggregator (with associated publishing rights cleared as well). What should I do? I don't want to take content down that should be up, but I also don't want the company to be subject to copyright infringement risk.

Answer: You are right to be concerned about this. The DMCA, however, puts the burden of managing copyright on the owners of such copyrights, and the law includes specific terms about how rights holders can assert such rights. ("The DMCA notification procedures place the burden of policing copyright infringement—identifying the potentially infringing material and adequately documenting the infringement—squarely on the owners of the copyright.")[2] In such a situation, it is nearly impossible for a distributor to know if the licensor of the content or the author of these demands for removal is the true owner of the associated

---

2 *Perfect 10 v. CCBill*, 488 F.3d 1102, 1113 (9th Cir. 2007)

copyright(s). A good first step in response to these notices is to review them all for compliance with the six-part takedown guidelines as set forth in section 512 of the Act. If the notices comply with the DMCA, you should take the content down until you can determine who is right. If they don't comply with the DMCA takedown guidelines (for example, they simply say that the use was not authorized), you can respond to the sender with a request for a DMCA compliant notice with a reference to your posted DMCA takedown policy (that you should definitely have, if you don't already). Often, the sixth component—requiring a statement under penalty of perjury that the sender has the right to the content and to demand its removal—will serve as an effective filter and will limit these notices to the legitimate ones. (You should also check your contracts with your sublicensor to ensure they indemnify you in the event they provide you infringing material.)

What about Rights in Different Territories?

Question: Why don't DMCA takedown notices require that the complainants specify the territory in which they want the content removed?

Answer: Some record labels and other licensors have rights on a territory-by-territory basis and may be able to demand takedown in the United States, but not Canada. Surprisingly, the DMCA is silent on territory. It is unknown whether this was a deliberate move or an accident. Until this is clarified, perhaps in a future amendment, the parties need to work together to ensure that takedowns are done in a manner that is the best for all parties involved, from both a legal and a business standpoint. This might mean tailoring takedowns to the specific demands of the sender and possibly even doing research to determine a licensor's territory rights.

These are just a few examples of how the DMCA comes into play in the music industry. Though the law is often criticized for making it too easy for distributors to simply remove content as a protective measure, it has served numerous other purposes fairly well and will continue to shape the way distributors and rights holders manage content online.

WHAT IS A DMCA "SAFE HARBOR"?

Title II of the DMCA, the Online Copyright Infringement Liability Limitation Act ("OCILLA"), creates what is known as a "safe harbor"—essentially, limitations on liability for monetary relief for those service providers that qualify. To qualify, ISPs and DSPs must qualify for and then adhere to certain prescribed safe harbor guidelines and promptly block access to allegedly infringing material if they receive a DMCA compliant notice. Such guidelines include: (1) adherence to a policy for the termination of service for repeat infringers, (2) accommodation of and noninterference with technical measures used to protect against infringement, (3) designation of a Copyright Agent, and (4) compliance with reasonably alleged takedown notices. In turn, an ISP can lose its safe harbor eligibility for the safe harbor if it (a) has actual or "red flag" knowledge of infringing activity on the service, and (b) "receive[s] a financial benefit directly attributable to the infringing activity, in a case in which the service provider has the right and ability to control such activity." [3]

EU SAFE HARBOR REFORMS

In 2019, the European Union adopted the 2019 Directive on Copyright in the Digital Single Market, which addressed a number of points, such as adding a "link tax" on digital publications. Important to music, Article 17 of the new directive, which must be transcribed into local law and implemented by member countries by mid 2021, largely removes the "safe-harbor" for user-generated services in the EU, and requires them to have a license for any material available on their platform, or to block the material:

> If no authorisation is granted, online content-sharing service providers shall be liable for unauthorised acts of communication to the public, including making available to the public, of copyright-protected works and other subject matter, unless the service providers demonstrate that they have:
>
> 1. (a) made best efforts to obtain an authorisation, and

---

3   17 U.S.C. § 512(c)(1)(B); § 512(d)(2)

2. *(b) made, in accordance with high industry standards of professional diligence, best efforts to ensure the unavailability of specific works and other subject matter for which the rightholders have provided the service providers with the relevant and necessary information; and in any event*

3. *(c) acted expeditiously, upon receiving a sufficiently substantiated notice from the rightholders, to disable access to, or to remove from, their websites the notified works or other subject matter, and made best efforts to prevent their future uploads in accordance with point (b). Chapter 2, Article 17, Directive (EU) 2019/790.*

In 2018, the U.S. safe harbor for ISPs was tested by the *BMG Rights Mgmt. (US) LLC v Cox Communications* case. The court in this case needed to consider whether internet service providers have a duty to police their subscribers in order to have safe harbor protection, and whether failure to terminate the accounts of repeat infringers could penetrate the safe harbor and allow an ISP to be held liable for the actions of a subscriber.

Rightscorp, a third party contracted by BMG to police infringement of BMG material, had over time sent numerous notices of repeat infringers to Cox, which had not taken action to terminate those accounts. There was a question as to who could actually adjudicate the "guilt" of a subscriber and whether Cox should merely take the word of Rightscorp in terminating accounts. The Courts of Appeals found that Cox failed to implement its own repeat infringer policy (which was a "13-strike policy", and remanded the case to lower court for a new trial, at which point Cox chose to settle the case. Cox later lost a case from Warner, Sony, and Universal in 2019 in which the plaintiffs were awarded $1 billion in statutory damages.

Blanket Licenses

Others have argued that perhaps an ISP flat fee is the best way to collect revenue lost to piracy. In 2009, the RIAA experimented with blanket licenses on college campuses through a program called Choruss. Staffed by Warner Music consultants, the company hoped to implement unlimited access to music for students at colleges that are part of the program, paid for through an increased student activity fee, although the program never made it beyond a conceptual phase.

Interactive streaming services have also actively partnered with mobile operators for bundled music. Orange, the French mobile operator, has a partnership with Deezer in several different countries, and Cricket Wireless in the U.S. now offers a bundle with Deezer as well. (Deezer took over for Muve Music in 2015.)

The role ISPs, in particular mobile operators, play in the distribution of music and other media will no doubt be an interesting area to watch in coming months and years.

CREATIVE COMMONS AND THE "COPYLEFT" MOVEMENT

While Congress and entertainment industry professionals argue about the best way to protect works, there are others on the other end of the spectrum who argue that the solution is to limit copyright protection. One of the first leaders of this "copyleft" movement was former Stanford and Harvard law professor Lawrence Lessig.

FIG. 12.1. The Copyleft Symbol

Lessig, the founder and former CEO of Creative Commons, has become the face and name of the "copyleft" movement. Together with the Creative Commons organization, he has successfully managed to break ground in establishing a new approach to copyright where creative works are more available to others to build new works upon. The heart of this idea lies in the "Creative Commons licenses," which allow for the creator to determine and communicate what exclusive rights they want to preserve and what exclusive rights they want to waive in releasing their creations to the public.

As an example, consider the following. The band Nine Inch Nails released *Ghosts I–IV* in 2008, a collection of thirty-six instrumental tracks licensed under a Creative Commons license that allowed users to remix and share the tracks with anyone, as long as they were not for commercial gain. Some thought this was innovative because it supported wide dissemination of the content, created buzz around the album, and actually seems to have encouraged sales. Some thought it was foolish because it supported the notion of "free" music and could subject the artist to a dramatic reduction in revenues stemming from album sales. Either way, it is an example of a new approach gaining traction in a new era of copyright.

Although Lessig has moved his practice to focus on corporate ethics (which perhaps emanates from his dealings with the music industry!), in his older commentary on piracy, Lessig points to a failed system of tracking copies on the Internet that could one day be changed with the advent of successful controlled access systems.

> *"Sales might go up, my reputation might go up (or down), but there is no way to trace the drop in sales to this individual theft, and no way to link the rise (or fall) in fame to this subsidized distribution.... So a system that controlled access in this more fine-grained way would grant access to its resources only to another system that controlled access in the same fine-grained way. A hierarchy of systems would develop; and copyright material would be traded only within that system that controlled access properly."* [4]

As Lessig pointed out in his book *Code: Version 2.0*, "An important point about copyright law is that, though designed in part to protect authors, the control it was designed to create was never meant to be perfect." [5] Fair use exceptions, and other limited terms mean that copyright is not an all-encompassing absolute right of an author. Consumers may also sell their copy of a book or CD, without payment of a royalty, under the first sale doctrine. (In the music industry, the sale of used CDs was a major issue for artists in the early 1990s, with Garth Brooks refusing to ship his CD *In Pieces* to stores dealing in used CDs until his actions were shut down as the result of an antitrust lawsuit against his label, Capitol Records.)

Lessig also made waves when he suggested an "alternative compensation system," a tax be levied at the ISP level to every consumer to help the shortfall in revenue due to piracy—one of the very systems now being considered. Payments could be calculated by tracking the traffic of music on the Internet via an embedded watermark placed by copyright holders into DRM-free music files, or other tracking mechanisms.

---

4   "The Law of the Horse: What Cyberlaw Might Teach." *Harvard Law Review*. 113: (1999), 501
5   Lessig, Lawrence. *Code: Version 2.0*. New York: Basic, 2006

The owner of the copyright in an audio or video recording who wished to be compensated when it was used by others would register it with the Copyright Office and would receive, in return, a unique file name, which then would be used to track its distribution, consumption, and modification. The government would raise the money necessary to compensate copyright owners through a tax most likely, a tax on the devices and services that consumers use to gain access to digital entertainment. Using techniques pioneered by television rating services and performing rights organizations, a government agency would estimate the frequency with which each song and film was listened to or watched. The tax revenues would then be distributed to copyright owners in proportion to the rates with which their registered works were being consumed." [6]

While the idea is interesting, implementation of such a major change in revenue structure will no doubt require years for debate, study of the impact, passage of legislation, and implementation of the technological systems, and by that time, the access model may have finally reached critical mass. And while the copyleft movement has received a great deal of publicity, it is opposed by many creators and industry organizations alike, although some parts of its plans may indeed come to fruition.

TRANSFER OF VALUE

Many people in the creative community have become concerned about the so-called "transfer of value"—the benefit in profit and stock price enjoyed by large technology companies like Google/YouTube, Apple, Facebook, and Amazon. Amazon, on the book side, has been widely criticized for their negotiating practices with authors and publishers. YouTube pays about 50 percent of their revenue out to rights holders, in comparison to Spotify and TIDAL's approximately 70 percent, even though they are a part of a large, very profitable public company. Rights holders argue that their hands are tied in negotiating procedures because user-generated companies can fall back on the safe harbor as a means of paying no royalties at all. As mentioned, the U.S. Copyright Office conducted an open call for comments on the safe harbor provision of the DMCA, and received more than 91,000 written remarks before the call closed. Changes have been considered or adopted in other countries as well, as we've seen with the 2019 EU Copyright

6   www.lessig.org/blog/2004/10/alternative_compensation_syste.html

Directive, given that technology (which didn't exist when safe harbor was originally passed) has come far enough to allow YouTube and user-generated content sites to scan and identify content when uploaded.

HOW MUCH DOES GLOBAL INTERNET PIRACY COST THE SOUND RECORDING INDUSTRY?

Analysis by the IFPI concludes that global sound recording piracy causes billions of lost revenue each year, resulting in job losses and lower artist payouts. Twenty percent of fixed-line Internet users regularly access services with infringing music.

CHAPTER 13

UGC, NFTs, AI, Livestreaming, and More

To copyright advocates, the newest generation of sites and services pose a whole new level of threat to conventional copyright protection. Now, not only can music (and any other copyrighted content) be copied and easily sent among users online, but users can post content to their own personal sites or pages, or on heavily trafficked user-generated content ("UGC") sites and applications like Tiktok. These sites allow users to build upon and interact with information or content, and often that means third-party-owned music content. Perhaps the largest examples of these now are YouTube and SoundCloud, which have negotiated blanket licenses with some record labels and publishers to cover the widespread use of their music on the sites.

So, are there different copyright rules that apply to such uses? Do users who post a song on their blog need a license from the rights holder(s)? Does the background music on my personal social networking page need to be licensed? The answer to these questions is yes, if the person posting the materials does not legally control the content. That said, there are still several to-be-answered questions in this area with case law and practice currently defining what is legal and acceptable.

WHAT CAN I POST TO YOUTUBE?

Question: I have a video of my daughter lip-synching a popular hip-hop song. Can I post this to YouTube without infringing anyone's copyright?

Answer: *Not necessarily. As was played out in the Lenz v. Universal case in the Northern District of California, there remain numerous unanswered questions with regard to copyright. The Lenz case came about when a mother posted a 29-second video of her child dancing to "Let's Go Crazy," a song recorded by Prince, the sound recording of which is licensed by Universal Records. Universal requested and obtained a takedown from YouTube, which was followed by the video being reposted by YouTube at Lenz's request using the little-used portion of the DMCA codified at 17 U.S.C. § 512(g)(3) (counter-notification pursuant to which the original poster states under penalty of perjury that they have "a good faith belief that the material was removed or disabled as a result of mistake or misidentification of the material to be removed or disabled"). Essentially, Lenz had sent YouTube a DMCA counter-notification taking the position that her video constituted a "fair use" of "Let's Go Crazy" and thus did not infringe any third-party copyrights. The video was reposted by YouTube after which Lenz utilized an even more rarely employed portion of the DMCA, 17 U.S.C. § 512(f), which provides for liability upon those who file DMCA notices without the requisite good faith belief that the material in question is an infringement of the copyright owner's rights. Universal's subsequent motion to dismiss was denied, setting some powerful precedent.* In a nutshell, rights holders issuing takedown notices have a duty to consider whether a use is a "fair use" just as much as a poster has a duty to consider whether a use is legal.

More recently the concept of livestreaming (the broadcast of live music performances online) has become more and more prevalent (with tremendous growth during the COVID-19 pandemic lockdowns of 2020). Livestreaming present a number of questions and challenges, and could require a number of licenses, including synchronization, master and mechanical user, name and likeness, and public performance—all depending on the type of music livestreamed and whether one plans to make a recording available afterwards. Facebook, Twitch, and Instagram all have terms of use requiring broadcasters to have the rights to include music in their livestreams, often this is impractical—since songs are often by request or chosen on the fly. If you plan to do a pay-per-view livestream using a platform like StageIt, you (or the platform) will need to clear the music rights with publishers and labels (if pre-recorded music is included) (and pay them part of the fees.)

Perceptions of UGC sites and applications often turn on whether one is a subscriber to the copyright or the copyleft movement. For the music industry, this generation of uses of the Internet spells increased opportunity for exposure and distribution alongside increased risk of economic loss. For optimists, the new era is shining a bright light on one area of copyright law that could likely benefit from reform. Perhaps it will be the increased prevalence of applications that will force the industry into a collectively agreed upon blanket license for noncommercial uses. Perhaps Creative Commons licenses will become more mainstream. No matter what, the rights of the original creators and those seeking to reuse or repurpose third party works are going to continue to need to be balanced against one another in Congress, the courts, and online.

Finally, no discussion of rapid technology developments for distribution would be complete without a mention of two very important and very rapidly developing technologies: NFTs (non-fungible tokens—unique digital assets whose ownership is tracked on the blockchain), and artificial intelligence (AI). NFTs, which exploded in early 2021 with multi-million dollar transactions for single pieces of art and music, allow their holder to be the confirmed (via blockchain immutability) owner of a specific piece of digital content and will likely be a key part of our evolving lives in the metaverse. However, while NFTs are a valiant effort to reintroduce scarcity into digital content, the fact remains that all digital content can be easily replicated—and this will raise all kinds of questions. Does the owner of the NFT "own" the copyright? In some cases, the NFT represents the copyright, and in some case the NFT represents the copy (which is generally meant to be of a limited amount). Separately, artificial intelligence is bringing a host of new discussions as well. Specifically, can a computer own the copyright in a song it writes? What about a joint work with a human? As of this writing, this is an issue that has not yet been widely concluded.

In the end, rights holders and others in the music industry should be viewing and treating new uses of musical content the same way one would treat other uses: all should be licensed or fall into a license exception (fair use, for example), or it cannot be legally used. There is currently no outright exception to copyright law for non-commercial uses, so whether music is posted on a private blog with three viewers or a popular UGC gaming site, copyright implications need to be carefully considered. Further, there is no blanket or wholesale licensing system available for such uses, so each use and each distinct piece of content is subject to its own copyright clearance or infringement analysis. The hope for many in the industry is that this will change with time, but to date, the law is moving slowly. Many believe that substantial change in business standards can only occur as a result of government intervention. Regardless of where one falls on the copyright/copyleft spectrum, the emergence of these uses of the Internet is going to further challenge copyright law as we know it in years to come.

WHO PAYS IF I UPLOAD TO SOUNDCLOUD?

Question: Wanton Success has covered a Johnny Cash tune and wants to post the song on their SoundCloud page. Under the compulsory license scheme, Wanton Success is entitled to a mechanical license at the statutory rate, as we discussed earlier. But is posting for streaming legal? Who pays the public performance and mechanical royalties for this, if SoundCloud is a free offering for artists?

Answer: *This is a thorny area. Theoretically, a stream includes both a mechanical and a public performance component. Mechanicals should be paid by the service under the CRB rates set in effect for streaming, and SoundCloud should have licenses in place with the PROs to cover the public performance of works. However, SoundCloud specifically requires users to certify that they are only uploading content they control. The site's terms of service also state that users warrant that content they upload does not violate the rights of a third party and that the* user *is responsible for the payment of royalties. (This is why you should always read the terms of service when joining an online service, even though most people just click "agree" and move on without a second thought.)*

So, in this case, unless Wanton Success specifically cleared the use with the Johnny Cash song's current owner or obtained assurance that SoundCloud will take responsibility for the licensing, Wanton Success should steer clear of uploading their version of the song to SoundCloud. If they do, SoundCloud may remove it.

MY SONGS ARE ON YOUTUBE, AND WHILE I RECEIVE PAYMENTS, I SEE MY MUSIC BEING USED IN ALL KINDS OF VIDEOS. DON'T YOUTUBE AND THE UPLOADER NEED A SYNCHRONIZATION LICENSE TO DO THIS?

Technically, yes, and while synchronization licenses are not compulsory under the law like a mechanical license, under the terms of another settlement reached by music publishers, YouTube has blanket synchronization licenses that allow publishers to opt in to receive up to 50 percent of the advertising revenue from a song on the service.

CHAPTER 14

Overseas Licensing/ Challenges of Operating in a Global Environment

EU DIRECTIVES FOR STANDARDIZATION

We've seen a number of the mechanisms employed in the United States and around the world for the protection of creative rights. However, what about licensing of music rights around the world? How does this work, given the complexities and differences in law between countries?

The European Union continues to push for harmonization of copyright laws in its member states via copyright directives. (Remember that copyright is still controlled locally, but the EU has the authority to offer direction on which laws should be imple-mented at the local level and how they should work.) The EU has been a much harsher critic than the U.S. of YouTube, Google, and large technology companies on issues around content and privacy. They have also released, for example, several directives on collective management of rights, and are currently considering the international portability of subscription accounts as part of their Single Digital Market initiative. (Ever traveled overseas and tried to access content on YouTube or Netflix, only to find that it's blocked in certain geographic regions based on IP address? That's one issue they're trying to solve, within Europe at least.) We may see continued regulation coming from the EU, the nature of which is bound to impact international copyright standards.

What are some of the key differences between U.S. copyright law and European laws? One of the most prevalent examples is the lack of a codified fair use defense outside the U.S.—meaning that defendants in a court case cannot rely on the vague "four prong" test used in the U.S. Rather, some countries have passed exceptions to copyright for specific uses.

Additionally, as discussed earlier, most countries in Europe have a single performing rights organization that licenses both reproduction (mechanical) rights and public performance rights for musical compositions, as well as public performance for sound recordings. (The Copyright Office advocated for such an arrangement in the U.S. in their 2015 report. Remember also that most countries in Europe provide for royalties to sound recording copyright holders for any public performance, not just digital transmissions as is the case in the United States.) Despite the aggregation of rights under one house in each country, this still means that currently 27 different performing rights organizations across Europe—one in each country—handle licensing of musical compositions and sound recordings. This has led to incredible difficulty in licensing works throughout Europe, as licensees must obtain licenses from each country's PRO.

In response, the European Commission issued a directive requiring performing rights organizations to find a way to grant licenses across the EU, meaning that rights holders can divide their rights (for example, physical vs. digital) between certain collecting societies. In response, we've seen developments like Warner/Chappell Music Group's Pan-European Digital Licensing initiative (PEDL) and ICE. The PEDL allows "one-stop" shopping for pan-European licenses, meaning there are certain PROs allowed by Warner/Chappell to grant licenses for their catalogue for use across all European territories (right now, BUMA, SACEM, SABAM, GEMA, STIM, and PRS for Music). A number of other publishers and European PROs continue to work on plans for their own pan-European licensing initiatives.

Another directive on collective rights management in the EU issued in 2014 called for greater reporting and transparency requirements of all European PROs. The directive also requires that European PROs treat non-members equally as their members, meaning that this directive has an immediate worldwide effect, since those PROs collect and account to non-members for European uses of their music.

Finally, as we already discussed, the EU took significant steps in 2019 to reform copyright, most notably providing additional paths for cross-border collective licensing and shrinking the scope of the safe harbor provision.

Will there be further initiatives in other regions to lessen the complications of music licensing in places like South America and Asia, as globalization continues? Only time will tell.

Clearing Rights in Multiple Territories

Due to the worldwide nature of the Internet, online music sites face their own range of challenges in ensuring that they comply with licensor-mandated territory restrictions. Some sites, such as iTunes, control access and licensing based on the IP address of the user or the address associated with a customer's credit card. However, illegitimate sites such as Pirate Bay and torrent sites generally do not seek to limit access on a territory-by-territory basis (for obvious reasons). Anybody with an interest in learning more about music law outside of the United States is encouraged to pursue research on a territory-by-territory basis. As a good starting point, we have compiled a list of the international collective licensing organizations and other international resources in appendix B.

CHAPTER 15

How to Start an Online Music Service

There are a range of considerations associated with starting a company that will legally distribute music via the Internet. I'll leave the fundamentals (funding, product offering, etc.) to the entrepreneurs and venture capitalists. From a licensing standpoint, the following are the steps one needs to take.

The market has revealed two primary ways to launch an online service that includes music: the legitimate, legal, and costly way, and the immediate, risky, and illegal way. Naturally, there are a number of success stories associated with each, but I do not advise or support anything other than a legal, legitimate approach to distributing copyrighted works, despite associated expense and hassle. While some may disagree, the problems and challenges faced in launching a new service will only persist if the business community is anything less than motivated to support positive change.

The immediate, risky, and illegal way to launch a service that includes music is to just do it without any (or at least, without all) required licenses. This is the "ask for forgiveness, not permission" tactic employed by a number of services launched in the past decade, including SoundCloud and YouTube. While it does not always work, the idea has proven fruitful in a few cases. The approach entails launching an offering and obtaining interest and traffic to the service to better your negotiating position. The hope is that while the rights holders have enormous leverage in later negotiations, they are not likely to shut the service down and are more interested in coming to deal terms, due to the potential revenue opportunity the service presents. In order to proceed with this approach, a company must have little to lose and substantial confidence in their offering; it has to be good enough to generate substantial attention and popularity extremely quickly. Note, however, that for each success story, there are perhaps hundreds of failures, many of which suffered enormous losses and litigation as a result of their reckless approach to distributing media without requisite licenses in place.

On the other hand, the legitimate, legal, and costly way to launch an online service that includes downloads and streams of music is to obtain all sound recording and composition licenses in advance of making the associated content available. This means getting (1) sound recording licenses for the masters from record labels (major and independent) and aggregators, (2) public performance licenses from the PROs (all three in the U.S.: ASCAP, BMI, and SESAC), (3) a blanket mechanical license from the MLC and any other voluntary licenses the services wishes to enter into for compositions underlying the masters you want to distribute, and (4) a license agreement in place with SoundExchange, if you want to include a DMCA compliant radio offering in your service. As you might guess, this process will likely take at least several months and be extremely costly, particularly when you consider legal and other professional fees, associated license fees (including advances), etc.

LICENSES REQUIRED

To start a legitimate digital download and online streaming service, one must obtain the following licenses:

1. sound recording licenses from record labels
2. public performance licenses from the PROs
3. a blanket mechanical license from the MLC and any other voluntary licenses the services wishes to enter into
4. sound recording licenses from SoundExchange, if you want to include a DMCA compliant radio offering in your service.

Due to the complicated nature of licensing music, particularly for online distribution, it takes a substantial investment to get into the industry. Some would argue that the convoluted licensing schemes are to blame for a weak catalog of service offerings for legal music. Some even argue that it is understandable that so many services go underground and choose to avoid the legal route altogether. The industry and all involved and invested in it would stand to gain a great deal if we could streamline the process by which a company can launch a legitimate, legal music service for which rights holders are properly paid.

Many argue that the way to go about this is to allow for a more thorough blanket-licensing scheme pursuant to which the quantity of required license agreements would go down due to a centralized clearinghouse mechanism of some kind. While this makes enormous sense, the industry has yet to make any significant progress in that direction. Solving the rights registry piece would also go a long way. Only time will tell if the cost of properly licensing is so prohibitive that the various stakeholders are forced to compromise for the greater good.

APPENDIX A

Abbreviations

ASCAP	American Society of Composers, Authors and Publishers
BMI	Broadcast Music, Inc.
CD	compact disc
CRB	Copyright Royalty Board
DAT	digital audio tape
DMCA	Digital Millennium Copyright Act
DPD	digital phonorecord delivery
DPRSRA	Digital Performance Right in Sound Recording Act
DRM	digital rights management
EU	European Union
HFA	Harry Fox Agency
IFPI	International Federation of the Phonographic Industry
IP	Internet protocol or intellectual property
ISP	Internet service provider
MLC	Mechanical Licensing Collective
MMA	Music Modernization Act
P2P	peer to peer
PRO	performing rights organization
RIAA	Recording Industry Association of America
SESAC	Society of European Stage Authors and Composers
UMG	Universal Music Group
WMG	Warner Music Group

Performing Rights Organizations and Related Companies

UNITED STATES

A2IM (American Association of Independent Music)
132 Delancey Street
New York, NY 10002
646-692-4877
www.a2im.org

AMRA Music
New York, NY
www.amra-music.com

ASCAP (American Society of Composers, Authors and Publishers)
1900 Broadway
New York, NY 10023
212-621-6000
(Many local offices nationwide)
www.ascap.com

BMI (Broadcast Music, Inc.)
7 World Trade Center
250 Greenwich Street
New York, NY 10007-0030
212-220-3000
(Many local offices nationwide)
www.bmi.com

Global Music Rights
www.globalmusicrights.com

Harry Fox Agency
40 Wall Street, 6th Floor
New York, NY 10005
212-834-0100
www.harryfox.com

Mechanical Licensing Collective
615-488-3653
www.themlc.com

RIAA (Recording Industry Association of America)
1025 F. Street NW, 10th Floor
Washington, DC 20004
202-775-0101
www.riaa.com

SESAC (Society of European Songwriters and Composers)
35 Music Square East
Nashville, TN 37203
615-320-0055
(Many local offices nationwide)
www.sesac.com

SoundExchange
733 10th Street NW, 10th Floor
Washington, DC 20001
202-640-5858
www.soundexchange.com

INTERNATIONAL PERFORMING RIGHTS ORGANIZATIONS

European Union

Buma/Stemra, the Netherlands—Represents the interests of music authors in the Netherlands.

- Makes sure they receive remuneration for the use of their creations.
- Works for composers, lyricists, and music publishers.
- Member of CISAC.
- www.bumastemra.nl

CEDAR (Musicopy), the Netherlands—Provides licenses to users for the use of sheet music (and lyrics) and pays the appropriate fee collected to the copyright owner and publisher.

www.cedar.nl

GEMA, Germany—One of the world's leading authors' societies for works of music.

- Offers customers the worldwide repertoire of music and provides services for all music authors and rights owners.
- Member of CISAC.
- www.gema.de

Gramex, Finland—Copyright society that promotes and administers the rights of performing artists whose performances have been recorded on phonograms and of producers of phonograms.

- Collects and distributes royalties owed.
- www.gramex.fi

GRAMO, Norway—Collects remuneration for performing artists and producers when their recordings are used for broadcasting and other public performances purposes.

- Represents performing artists and producers.
- Established in 1989.
- www.gramo.no

ICE (International Copyright Enterprise)—Joint venture between PRS for Music, STIM, and GEMA for pan-European licensing.

- Established in 2010.
- www.iceservices.com

PPI (Phonographic Performance Ireland), Ireland—Established in 1968 to act as a central administrator of record company rights in the public performance, broadcasting, and reproduction of their recordings.

- PPI collects money for when the recordings or music videos are played in public under a single license fee.
- www.ppiltd.com

PRS for Music—Exists to collect and pay royalties to its members when their music is recorded and made available to the public (MCPS), and when their music is performed, broadcast, or otherwise made publicly available (PRS for Music).

- Formed in 1997 between two royalty collection societies (MCPS and PRS).
- Money is generated (through license fees) from the recording of members' music on many different formats, including CDs, DVDs, television, broadcast, and online.
- Collects for any public performance of music, whether live or recorded, that takes place outside the home and from radio and television broadcasts and online.
- 10 million pieces of music.
- Member of CISAC.
- www.prsformusic.com

PPL (Phonographic Performance Limited)—Music industry organization collecting and distributing airplay and public performance royalties in the U.K. on behalf of over 3,500 record companies and 47,000 performers.

- Issues licenses to U.K. radio and television stations, other broadcasters, and Internet radio stations that use sound recordings in their transmissions.
- Also licenses clubs, shops, pubs, restaurants, and thousands of other music users who play sound recordings in public.
- www.ppluk.com

SACEM (Société des Auteurs, Compositeurs et Editeurs de Musique), France—Collects payments of authors' rights and redistributes them to the original authors, composers, and the publishers.

- Stated objective to look after the reproduction and performance rights of composers.
- Member of CISAC.
- www.sacem.fr

SCPP (Société civile des Producteurs Phonographiques), France—Collects fees due to its members from sound recording and music video users, and distributes these fees to copyright holders.

- Responsible for the collective administration and protection of record and video producers' rights since 1985.
- More than 1000 producers belong, including many independents and international majors including EMI, Warner, Universal, and Sony BMG.
- www.scpp.fr

SENA, the Netherlands—Appointed by the Ministry of Justice, and to the exclusion of any other, SENA has been charged with the execution of part of the Neighbouring Rights Act in 1993.

- Grants licenses to "users" of music for the public use of released phonograms for commercial purposes.

- SENA collects remunerations and, on the basis of legally approved regulations, pays them through to the performing artists and record producers.

- www.sena.nl

SIAE (Italian Society of Authors and Publishers), Italy—Italian law establishes that those who wish to organize shows or entertainments where intellectual works are exploited should procure a license from SIAE and pay the relative amount.

- Established in 1882, recognized officially by copyright law of 1941.

- Presently represents well over 50,000 authors and artists.

- Member of CISAC.

- www.siae.it

STIM (Swedish Performing Rights Society), Sweden—Protects the interests of authors and publishers of music in Sweden.

- On their behalf, STIM administers and licenses rights to music and text.

- Through its international network, STIM also represents rights of the worldwide repertoire of musical works.

- Member of CISAC.

- www.stim.se

SUISA (Swiss Cooperative Society for Authors and Publishers), Switzerland—Established in 1923, it now numbers about 25,000 composers, lyricists, and music publishers.

- Collects royalties for the public use of the works in Switzerland and Liechtenstein.

- Through reciprocity agreements with over 100 sister societies worldwide, SUISA manages the rights of 2 million rights holders.

- Manages "small rights," including non-dramatic musical works, concert versions of dramatic works, and musical works for feature and television films.

- Member of CISAC.

- www.suisa.ch

Teosto, Finland—Copyright organization for composers, lyric writers, arrangers, and music publishers.

- More than 19,000 music author and publisher members representing some two million rights holders around the world.

- Member of CISAC.

- www.teosto.fi

TONO, Norway—Grants license for performing music in public; collects money for the composers of music.

- Established in 1928.

- Protects the performing (financial and legal) rights of Norwegian and foreign composers, authors, and publishers of music.

- Member of CISAC.

- www.tono.no

ZPAV (Związek Producentów Audio Video), Poland—Founded in 1991 to represent the interests of legitimate music producers against piracy.

- Polish National Group of IFPI.

- Associates nearly 100 industry representatives and approximately 40 record companies.

- www.zpav.pl

INTERNATIONAL TRADE ASSOCIATIONS

BIEM (Bureau International des Sociétés Gérant les Droits d'Enregistrement et de Reproduction Mécanique)—International organization representing mechanical rights societies.

- Licenses the reproduction of songs.

- Based in France, formed in 1929.

- Represents 50 societies from 53 countries.

- Members of BIEM enter into agreements to allow each of them to represent the others' repertoire. In this way, a BIEM society is able to license users for the vast majority of protected works in the world.

- Collaborates with the international organizations that pursue the same objective, including CISAC and GESAC.

- www.biem.org

CISAC (International Confederation of Societies of Authors and Composers)—Works toward increased recognition and protection of creators' rights.

- Founded in 1926, non-governmental, non-profit organi-zation, headquartered in Paris.

- As of 2015, CISAC numbered 230 authors' societies from 120 countries and indirectly represents more than 4 million creators within all the artistic repertoires.

- Total amount of royalties collected by CISAC's member societies amount in 2014 to more than £7.9 billion.

- Main Activities and Services aim to:

    - Strengthen and develop the international network of copyright societies, and manage adherence to common standards.

    - Secure a position for creators and their collective man-agement organizations in the international scene.

- Adopt and implement quality and technical efficiency criteria to increase copyright societies' interoperability.

- Support societies' strategic development in each region and in each repertoire.

- Retain a central database allowing societies to exchange information efficiently.

- Participate in improving national and international copyright law and practices.

- www.cisac.org

GESAC (European Grouping of Societies of Authors and Composers)—Created in 1990, GESAC groups thirty-four of the largest authors' societies in European Union, Norway, and Switzerland.

- Represents nearly 500,000 authors or their successors in title in the area of music, graphic and plastic arts, literary and dramatic works, and audiovisual as well as music publishers.

- www.authorsocieties.eu

IFPI (International Federation of the Phonographic Industry)—Represents the recording industry worldwide, with a membership of some 1,400 record companies in 73 countries and affiliated industry associations in 48 countries.

- Mission is to promote the value of recorded music, safeguard the rights of record producers, and expand the commercial uses of recorded music in all markets where its members operate.

- Members include Universal, Sony Music, Warner Music Group, Beggars, and many other independents.

- www.ifpi.org

IFRRO (International Federation of Reproduction Rights Organisations)—Established to foster the fundamental inter-national copyright principles embodied in the Berne and Universal Copyright Conventions.

- Purpose is to facilitate, on an international basis, the collective management of reproduction and other rights relevant to copyrighted works through the cooperation of national reproduction rights organizations.

- Links RROs together around the world.

- Began in 1980 as a working group of the Copyright committee of the International Publishers Association and the International Group of Scientific, Technical, and Medical Publishers.

- www.ifrro.org

APPENDIX C

A&M Records, Inc. v. Napster, 239 F.3d 1004 (9th Cir. 2001, excerpted)

Numerous guiding principles were derived from the Ninth Circuit opinion, including the following three particularly relevant guidelines:

1. The free, unlicensed downloading of a complete audio file as a "sample" does not qualify for a fair use defense.

"5(a). Sampling

Napster contends that its users download MP3 files to "sample" the music in order to decide whether to purchase the recording. Napster argues that the district court: (1) erred in concluding that sampling is a commercial use because it conflated a noncommercial use with a personal use; (2) erred in determining that sampling adversely affects the market for plaintiff's copyrighted music, a requirement if the use is noncommercial; and (3) erroneously concluded that sampling is not a fair use because it determined that samplers may also engage in other infringing activity.

The district court determined that sampling remains a commercial use even if some users eventually purchase the music. We find no error in the district court's determination. Plaintiffs have established that they are likely to succeed in proving that even authorized temporary downloading of individual songs for sampling purposes is commercial in nature. The record supports a finding that free promotional downloads are highly regulated by the record company plaintiffs and that the companies collect royalties for song samples available on retail Internet sites. Evidence relied on by the district court demonstrates that the free downloads provided by the record companies consist of thirty- to sixty-second samples or are full songs programmed to "time out," that is, exist only for a short time on the downloader's computer. In comparison, Napster users download a full, free, and permanent copy of the recording. The determination by the district court as to the commercial purpose and character of sampling is not clearly erroneous.

The district court further found that both the market for audio CDs and market for online distribution are adversely affected by Napster's service. As stated in the discussion of the district court's general fair use analysis: the court did not abuse its discretion when it found that, overall, Napster has an adverse impact on the audio CD and digital download markets. Contrary to Napster's assertion that the district court failed to specifically address the market impact of sampling, the district court determined that "even if the type of sampling supposedly done on Napster were a noncommercial use, plaintiffs have demonstrated a substantial likelihood that it would adversely affect the potential market for their copyrighted works if it became widespread."

The record company supports the district court's preliminary determinations that: (1) the more music that sampling users download, the less likely they are to eventually purchase the recordings on audio CD; and (2) even if the audio CD market is not harmed, Napster has adverse effects on the developing digital download market."

.....

2. Napster's space-shifting is not fair use. *Space-shifting* (the practice of downloading an MP3 file of a track already owned on a CD for listening elsewhere) was yet another feature of the Napster service that was deemed not eligible for a fair use defense—a defense that had been successfully applied to other contexts (such as VHS videotapes).

"b. Space-shifting

Napster also maintains that space-shifting is a fair use. Space-shifting occurs when a Napster user downloads MP3 music files in order to listen to music he already owns on audio CD. Napster asserts that we have already held that space-shifting of musical compositions and sound recordings is a fair use.... We conclude that the district court did not err when it refused to apply the "shifting" analyses of Sony and Diamond. Both Diamond and Sony are inapposite because the methods of shifting in these cases did not also simultaneously involve distribution of the copyright material to the general public; the time or space-shifting of copyrighted material exposed the material only to the original user. In Diamond, for example, the copyrighted material was transferred from the user's computer hard drive to the user's portable MP3 player. So too Sony, where "the majority of VCR purchasers did not distribute taped television broadcasts, but merely enjoyed them at home."

Conversely it is obvious that once a user lists a copy of music he already owns on the Napster system in order to access the music from another location, the song becomes 'available to millions of other individuals,' not just the original CD owner. See UMG Recordings, 92 F.Supp.2d at 351-352 (finding space-shifting of MP3 files is not a fair use even when previous ownership is demonstrated before a download is allowed)."

3. A distributor can be held to be a "vicarious infringer" for failure to control or stop infringing activities when they are financially benefiting and have the ability to supervise, but do not do so. Because Napster failed to actively police their users, the company could be held liable for vicarious infringement.

"*IV.*

A. Knowledge

Contributory liability requires that the secondary infringer "know or have reason to know" of direct infringement. The district court found that Napster had both actual and constructive knowledge that its users exchanged copyrighted music. The district court also concluded that the law does not require knowledge of "specific acts of infringement" and rejected Napster's contention that because the company cannot distinguish infringing from non-infringing files, it does not "know" of the direct infringement.

It is apparent from the record that Napster has knowledge, both actual and constructive, of direct infringement. Napster claims that it is nevertheless protected from contributory liability by the teaching of Sony Corp. v. Universal City Studios, Inc. 464 U.S. 417 (1984). We disagree. We observe that Napster's actual, specific knowledge of direct infringement renders Sony's holding of limited assistance to Napster. We are compelled to make a clear distinction between the architecture of the Napster system and Napster's conduct in relation to the operational capacity of the system.

…The record supports the district court's finding that Napster has actual knowledge that specific infringing material is available using its system, that it could block access to the system by supplier of the infringing material, and that it failed to remove the material.

B. Material contribution

Under the facts as found by the district court, Napster materially contributes to the infringing activity. Relying on Fonovisa v. Cherry Auction, 76 F.Ed 259 (9th Cir. 1996), the district court concluded that "without the support services defendant provides, Napster users could not find and download the music they want with the ease of which defendant boasts." Napster, 114 F.Supp.2d at 919-20 ("Napster is an integrated service designed to enable users to locate and download MP3 music files."). We agree that Napster provides "the site and facilities" for direct infringement. The district court correctly applied the reasoning in Fonovisa, and properly found that Napster materially contributes to direct infringement.

V.

We turn to the question whether Napster engages in vicarious copyright infringement. Vicarious copyright liability is an "outgrowth" of respondeat superior. Fonovisa, 76 F.3d at 262. In the context of copyright law, vicarious liability extends beyond an employer/employee relationship to cases in which a defendant "has the right and ability to supervise the infringing activity and also has a direct financial interest in such activities." Id. (quoting Gershwin, 443 F.2d at 1162); see also Polygram Int'l Publ'g, Inc. v. Nevada/TIG, Inc., 855 F. Supp. 1314, 1325-26 (D. Mass. 1994) (describing vicarious liability as a form of risk allocation).

A. Financial benefit

The district court determined that plaintiffs had demonstrated they would likely succeed in establishing that Napster has a direct financial interest in the infringing activity. Napster, 114 F. Supp. 2d at 921-22. We agree. Financial benefit exists where the availability of infringing material "acts as a 'draw' for customers." Fonovisa, 76 F.3d at 263-64 (stating that financial benefit may be shown "where infringing performances enhance the attractiveness of a venue"). Ample evidence supports the district court's finding that Napster's future revenue is directly dependent upon "increases in userbase." More users register with the Napster system as the "quality and quantity of available music increases." 114 F. Supp. 2d at 902. We conclude that the district court did not err in determining that Napster financially benefits from the availability of protected works on its system.

B. Supervision

The district court determined that Napster has the right and ability to supervise its users' conduct. Napster, 114 F. Supp. 2d at 920-21 (finding that Napster's representations to the court regarding "its improved methods of blocking users about whom rights holders complain . . . is tantamount to an admission that defendant can, and sometimes does, police its service"). We agree in part.

The ability to block infringers' access to a particular environment for any reason whatsoever is evidence of the right and ability to supervise. See Fonovisa, 76 F.3d at 262 ("Cherry Auction had the right to terminate vendors for any reason whatsoever and through that right had the ability to control the activities of *vendors on the premises.");* cf. *Netcom,* 907 F. *Supp. at 1375-76 (indicating that plaintiff raised a genuine issue of fact regarding ability to supervise by presenting evidence that an electronic bulletin board service can suspend subscriber accounts). Here, plaintiffs have demonstrated that Napster retains the right to control access to its system. Napster has an express reservation of rights policy, stating on its website that it expressly reserves the "right to refuse service and terminate accounts in [its] discretion, including, but not limited to, if Napster believes that user conduct violates applicable law . . . or for any reason in Napster's sole discretion, with or without cause."*

To escape imposition of vicarious liability, the reserved right to police must be exercised to its fullest extent. Turning a blind eye to detectable acts of infringement for the sake of profit gives rise to liability. ....The district court correctly determined that Napster had the right and ability to police its system and failed to exercise that right to prevent the exchange of copyrighted material. The district court, however, failed to recognize that the boundaries of the premises that Napster "controls and patrols" are limited. See, e.g., Fonovisa, 76 F.2d at 262-63 (in addition to having the right to exclude vendors, defendant "controlled and patrolled" the premises); see also Polygram, 855 F. Supp. at 1328-29 (in addition to having the contractual right to remove exhibitors, trade show operator reserved the right to police during the show and had its "employees walk the aisles to ensure 'rules compliance'"). Put differently, Napster's reserved "right and ability" to police is cabined by the system's current architecture. As shown by the record, the Napster system does not "read" the content of indexed files, other than to check that they are in the proper MP3 format.

Napster, however, has the ability to locate infringing material listed on its search indices, and the right to terminate users' access to the system. The file name indices, therefore, are within the "premises" that Napster has the ability to police. We recognize that the files are user-named and may not match copyrighted material exactly (for example, the artist or song could be spelled wrong). For Napster to function effectively, however, file names must reasonably or roughly correspond to the material contained in the files, otherwise no user could ever locate any desired music. As a practical matter, Napster, its users, and the record company plaintiffs have equal access to infringing material by employing

Napster's "search function." Our review of the record requires us to
accept the district court's conclusion that plaintiffs have demonstrated a likelihood of success on the merits of the vicarious copyright infringement claim. Napster's failure to police the system's
"premises," combined with a showing that Napster financially
benefits from the continuing availability of infringing files on its
system, leads to the imposition of vicarious liability. We address
the scope of the injunction in part VIII of this opinion."

4. Napster attempted to raise two defenses to the infringement
   claim, but the court found that neither the safe harbor provision
   of the Digital Millennium Copyright Act protected the company
   from liability, nor that Napster users' actions are not protected
   by the Audio Home Recording Act of 1992.

"VI

Napster alleges that two statutes insulate it from liability. First,
Napster asserts that its users engage in actions protected by
§ 1008 of the Audio Home Recording Act of 1992, 17 U.S.C. §
1008. Second, Napster argues that its liability for contributory
and vicarious infringement is limited by the Digital Millennium
Copyright Act, 17 U.S.C. § 512. We address the application of each
statute in turn.

A. Audio Home Recording Act

We agree with the district court that the Audio Home Recording
Act does not cover the downloading of MP3 files to computer
hard drives. First, "[u]nder the plain meaning of the Act's definition of digital audio recording devices, computers (and their
hard drives) are not digital audio recording devices because their
'primary purpose' is not to make digital audio copied recordings."
Recording Indus. Ass'n of Am. v. Diamond Multimedia Sys., Inc.,
180 F.3d 1072, 1078 (9th Cir. 1999). Second, notwithstanding
Napster's claim that computers are "digital audio recording
devices," computers do not make "digital music recordings" as
defined by the Audio Home Recording Act. Id. at 1077 (citing S.
Rep. 102-294) ("There are simply no grounds in either the plain
language of the definition or in the legislative history for inter-
preting the term 'digital musical recording' to include songs fixed
on computer hard drives.").

B. Digital Millennium Copyright Act

Napster also interposes a statutory limitation on liability by asserting the protections of the "safe harbor" from copyright infringement suits for "Internet service providers" contained in the Digital Millennium Copyright Act, 17 U.S.C. § 512. See Napster, 114 F. Supp. 2d at 919 n.24. The district court did not give this statutory limitation any weight favoring a denial of temporary injunctive relief. The court concluded that Napster "has failed to persuade this court that subsection 512(d) shelters contributory infringers." Id....

Plaintiffs have raised and continue to raise significant questions under this statute, including: (1) whether Napster is an Internet service provider as defined by 17 U.S.C. § 512(d); (2) whether copyright owners must give a service provider "official" notice of infringing activity in order for it to have knowledge or awareness of infringing activity on its system; and (3) whether Napster complies with § 512(i), which requires a service provider to timely establish a detailed copyright compliance policy. See A&M Records, Inc. v. Napster, Inc., No. 99-05183, 2000 WL 573136 (N.D. Cal. May 12, 2000) (denying summary judgment to Napster under a different subsection of the Digital Millennium Copyright Act, § 512(a)).

The district court considered ample evidence to support its determination that the balance of hardships tips in plaintiffs' favor:

Any destruction of Napster, Inc. by a preliminary injunction is speculative compared to the statistical evidence of massive, unauthorized downloading and uploading of plaintiffs' copyrighted works–as many as 10,000 files per second by defendant's own admission. See Kessler Dec. ¶ 29. The court has every reason to believe that, without a preliminary injunction, these numbers will mushroom as Napster users, and newcomers attracted by the publicity, scramble to obtain as much free music as possible before trial. 114 F. Supp. 2d at 926.

VIII

The district court correctly recognized that a preliminary injunction against Napster's participation in copyright infringement is not only warranted but required. We believe, however, that the scope of the injunction needs modification in light of our opinion. Specifically, we reiterate that contributory liability may potentially be imposed only to the extent that Napster: (1) receives reasonable knowledge of specific infringing files with copyrighted musical compositions and sound recordings; (2) knows or should know that such files are available on the Napster system; and (3) fails to act to prevent viral distribution of the works. See Netcom, 907 F. Supp. at 1374-75. The mere existence of the Napster system, absent actual notice and Napster's demonstrated failure to remove the offending material, is insufficient to impose contributory liability. See Sony, 464 U.S. at 442-43.

There was a preliminary determination here that Napster users are not fair users. Uses of copyrighted material that are not fair uses are rightfully enjoined. See Dr. Seuss Enters. v. Penguin Books USA, Inc., 109 F.3d 1394, 1403 (9th Cir. 1997) (rejecting defendants' claim that injunction would constitute a prior restraint in violation of the First Amendment).

IX

The Copyright Act provides for various sanctions for infringers. See, e.g., 17 U.S.C. § 502 (injunctions); 504 (damages); and 506 (criminal penalties); see also 18 U.S.C. § 2319A (criminal penalties for the unauthorized fixation of and trafficking in sound recordings and music videos of live musical performances). These statutory sanctions represent a more than adequate legislative solution to the problem created by copyright infringement.

Imposing a compulsory royalty payment schedule would give Napster an "easy out" of this case. If such royalties were imposed, Napster would avoid penalties for any future violation of an injunction, statutory copyright damages, and any possible criminal penalties for continuing infringement. The royalty structure would also grant Napster the luxury of either choosing to continue and pay royalties or shut down. On the other hand, the wronged parties would be forced to do business with a company that profits from the wrongful use of intellectual properties. Plaintiffs would lose the power to control their intellectual property: they could not make a business decision not to license their property to Napster, and, in the event they planned to do business with Napster, compulsory royalties would take away the copyright holders' ability to negotiate the terms of any contractual arrangement.

We affirm in part, reverse in part, and remand. We direct that the preliminary injunction fashioned by the district court prior to this appeal shall remain stayed until it is modified by the district court to conform to the requirements of this opinion. We order a partial remand of this case on the date of the filing of this opinion for the limited purpose of permitting the district court to proceed with the settlement and entry of the modified preliminary injunction.

Even though the preliminary injunction requires modification, appellees have substantially and primarily prevailed on appeal. Appellees shall recover their statutory costs on appeal. See Fed. R. App. P. 39(a)(4) ('[i]f a judgment is affirmed in part, reversed in part, modified, or vacated, costs are taxed only as the court orders.')."

Metro-Goldwyn-Mayer Studios Inc., et al. v. Grokster, Ltd., 545 U.S. 913 (2005, excerpted)

The question addressed by the Court was, "Under what circumstances is the distributor of a product capable of both lawful and unlawful use liable for the acts of copyright infringement by third parties using the product?" The Court described the history of the products and the companies' promotion for illegitimate purposes before holding that those who distribute and promote an object that fosters infringement can be held liable for the infringing acts of its users (third parties):

> "Grokster and StreamCast are not, however, merely passive recipients of information about infringing use. The record is replete with evidence that from the moment Grokster and StreamCast began to distribute their free software, each one clearly voiced the objective that recipients use it to download copyrighted works, and each took active steps to encourage infringement. After the notorious file-sharing service, Napster, was sued by copyright holders for facilitation of copyright infringement, A & M Records, Inc. v. Napster, Inc., 114 F. Supp. 2d 896 (ND Cal. 2000), aff'd in part, rev'd in part, 239 F. 3d 1004 (CA9 2001), StreamCast gave away a software program of a kind known as OpenNap, designed as compatible with the Napster program and open to Napster users for downloading files from other Napster and OpenNap users' computers. Evidence indicates that it was always StreamCast's intent to use

its OpenNap network to be able to capture email addresses of its initial target market so that it could promote its Stream-Cast Morpheus interface to them, . . . An internal email from a company executive stated: 'We have put this network in place so that when Napster pulls the plug on their free service . . . or if the Court orders them shut down prior to that . . . we will be positioned to capture the flood of their 32 million users that will be actively looking for an alternative'. . . .

Finally, there is no evidence that either company made an effort to filter copyrighted material from users' downloads or otherwise impede the sharing of copyrighted files. Although Grokster appears to have sent emails warning users about infringing content when it received threatening notice from the copyright holders, it never blocked anyone from continuing to use its software to share copyrighted files. StreamCast not only rejected another company's offer of help to monitor infringement, but blocked the Internet Protocol addresses of entities it believed were trying to engage in such monitoring on its networks. . . .

. . . The argument for imposing indirect liability in this case is, however, a powerful one, given the number of infringing downloads that occur every day using StreamCast's and Grokster's software. When a widely shared service or product is used to commit infringement, it may be impossible to enforce rights in the protected work effectively against all direct infringers, the only practical alternative being to go against the distributor of the copying device for secondary liability on a theory of contributory or vicarious infringement. . . .

Evidence of active steps. . . taken to encourage direct infringement, Oak Industries, Inc. v. Zenith Electronics Corp., 697 F. Supp. 988, 992 (ND Ill. 1988), such as advertising an infringing use or instructing how to engage in an infringing use, show an affirmative intent that the product be used to infringe, and a showing that infringement was encouraged overcomes the law's reluctance to find liability when a defendant merely sells a commercial product suitable for some lawful use, see, e.g., Water Technologies Corp. v. Calco, Ltd., 850 F. 2d 660, 668 (CA Fed. 1988) (liability for inducement where one actively and knowingly aids and abets another's direct infringement. . .). For the same reasons that Sony took the staple-article doctrine of patent law as a model for its copyright safe-harbor rule, the inducement rule, too, is a sensible one for copyright. We adopt it here, holding that one who distributes a device with the object of promoting its use to infringe copyright, as shown by clear expression or other affirmative steps taken to foster infringement, is liable for the resulting acts of infringement by third parties.

....

Three features of this evidence of intent are particularly notable. First, each company showed itself to be aiming to satisfy a known source of demand for copyright infringement, the market comprising former Napster users. .... Second, this evidence of unlawful objective is given added significance by MGM's showing that neither company attempted to develop filtering tools or other mechanisms to diminish the infringing activity using their software. While the Ninth Circuit treated the defendants' failure to develop such tools as irrelevant because they lacked an independent duty to monitor their users' activity, we think this evidence underscores Grokster's and StreamCast's intentional facilitation of their users' infringement.... Third, there is a further complement to the direct evidence of unlawful objective. It is useful to recall that StreamCast and Grokster make money by selling advertising space, by directing ads to the screens of computers employing their software. As the record shows, the more the software is used, the more ads are sent out and the greater the advertising revenue becomes. Since the extent of the software's use determines the gain to the distributors, the commercial sense of their enterprise turns on high-volume use, which the record shows is infringing.... The unlawful objective is unmistakable.

...

In addition to intent to bring about infringement and distribution of a device suitable for infringing use, the inducement theory of course requires evidence of actual infringement by recipients of the device, the software in this case. As the account of the facts indicates, there is evidence of infringement on a gigantic scale, and there is no serious issue of the adequacy of MGM's showing on this point in order to survive the companies' summary judgment requests. Although an exact calculation of infringing use, as a basis for a claim of damages, is subject to dispute, there is no question that the summary judgment evidence is at least adequate to entitle MGM to go forward with claims for damages and equitable relief." [1]

---

1 *Metro-Goldwyn-Mayer Studios Inc., Et Al. v. Grokster, Ltd.*, 545 U.S. 913 (2005)

Payment Flows in Digital Music

Musical composition and sound recording copyright holders each have a number of potential revenue streams. In addition, download and subscription services see money flow in from consumers (and advertisers, if the service includes advertisements), and then pay some of such revenues back out to the copyright holders from whom they've licensed the music they make available on their sites. The following charts should give you a better idea of how the money flows.

REVENUE STREAMS FOR A WRITER/PUBLISHER

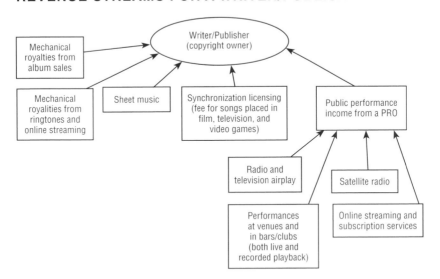

FIG. E.1. Revenue Streams for a Writer/Music Publisher

RECORD LABEL/REVENUE STREAMS FOR A SOUND RECORDING COPYRIGHT OWNER

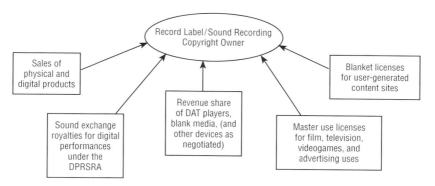

FIG. E.2. Cash Flows for a Download Service

Payment Flow Example: Beyoncé's "Baby Boy"

Let's examine one song: "Baby Boy" by Beyoncé, featuring Sean Paul. The following figures show the complexities of artists, writers, labels, and publishers sharing funds.

PROs

	Songwriters	Publishers
ASCAP	Shawn C. Carter	Beyoncé Publishing
	Sean Hennares	Black Owned Musik
	Beyoncé Gisselle Knowles	Carter Boys Music
	Sean Paul	Hitco South
	Scott Spencer Storch	Lil Lulu Publishing
	Robert G. Waller	Notting Dale Songs
		Reservoir Media Music
		Universal Music Corp
BMI	Kamoze Ini	Hattis Music Group
		Irving Music

Sound Exchange

Record Label	Featured Artists	Backing Musicians
Columbia Records	Beyoncé Gisselle Knowles **Sean Paul**	[Many!]

PP   *Public performance* revenue, which flows back to publishers and songwriters

MR   *Mechanical royalty* revenue, which flows back to publishers and songwriters

SR   *Sound recording* revenue, which flows back to record labels and recording artists

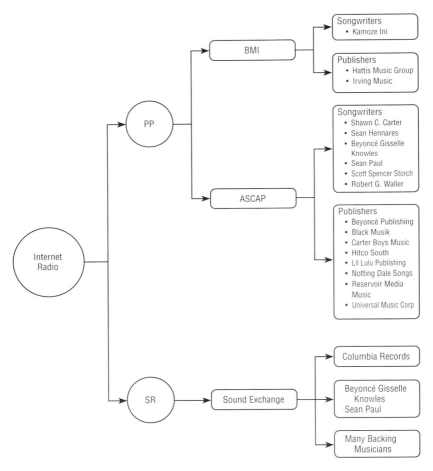

FIG. E.3. Internet Radio (e.g., NPR, Pandora, Sirius XM)

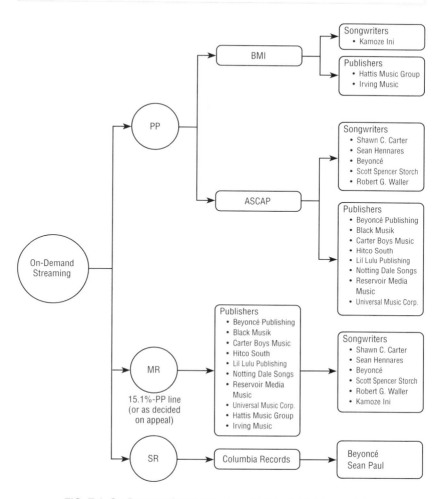

FIG. E.4. On-Demand Streaming (e.g., Spotify, Tidal, Rhapsody)

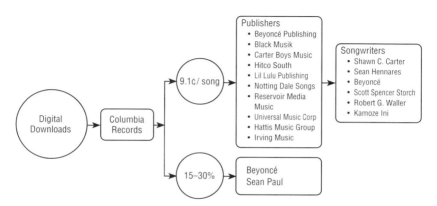

FIG. E.5. Digital Downloads (e.g., iTunes, Amazon, Google Play)

Helpful Documents

ARTIST CHECKLIST

As you probably gather, there is a long list of concerns for copyright holders and creators to consider. If you are an artist, here are few things to keep in mind:

✓ Register your sound recording copyrights at www.copyright.gov.

✓ Be sure to have assignment of copyright interest from any producers, hired studio musicians, or others who worked on your album.

✓ Join a PRO to collect performance royalties on public performances of your work(s).

✓ Make sure you have mechanical licenses in place for any songs you didn't write.

✓ Clear licenses with publishers and labels for any sampling.

✓ For distribution of your music online, content aggregators such as CD Baby, TuneCore, and the Orchard offer the ability to get your music onto services such as Spotify and iTunes without a record label.

✓ Join SoundExchange to receive royalties from digital performances.

✓ Stay on top of any agreements you enter into with labels, promoters, etc. Be aware of termination dates, promotional commitments, your right to leave a label, etc.

SONGWRITER CHECKLIST

Songwriters also have their share of work to do to ensure they are protected and can earn money from their musical compositions via recording and public performances. If you are a songwriter, here are few things to keep in mind:

✓ If you co-wrote a song, be sure to talk to your co-writers about the split of copyright ownership, and set it forth in writing.

✓ Register your musical composition copyrights at www .copyright.gov.

✓ Join a PRO, and set up both writer and publisher accounts.

✓ Register with the Mechanical Licensing Collective (MLC) to collect mechanical royalties in the U.S.

SAMPLE DMCA TAKEDOWN NOTICE

As discussed in chapter 12, a DMCA takedown notice can be sent to online sites demanding removal of materials you believe are infringing. The following is a good example of a DMCA takedown notice:

SAMPLE DMCA TAKEDOWN NOTICE

Date

Company Name

Address

Subject: Notice of Copyright Infringement

I am writing to provide you with a DMCA takedown notice for content appearing on your site. The copyrighted work at issue is [name of work] which appears on my pages at www.mycontent.com/page.html and www.mycontent.com/page2.html.

The URLs where our copyrighted material is located include www.website.com/abc .html and www.website.com/xyz.com. We hereby demand that you immediately remove this content from your site and provide us with an accounting of any and all distributions thereof to date.

You can reach me via email or phone for further information or clarification. My phone number is +1-202-555-1212. My mailing address is John Doe, 123 Centre Street, Boston, MA 02118.

I have a good faith belief that use of the copyrighted materials described above as allegedly infringing is not authorized by the copyright owner, its agent, or the law, and request that you remove the content.

I swear, under penalty of perjury, that the information in the notification is accurate and that I am the copyright owner or am authorized to act on behalf of the owner of an exclusive right that is allegedly infringed.

Sincerely,

YOUR NAME

INDEX

ABOUT THE AUTHOR

Photo by David Bacher

Allen Bargfrede focuses his work on the intersection of creative arts and technology. An American lawyer, he leads the media strategy firm Avance Advisors, and actively works with various American and European music and technology companies on business, strategy, investments, and policy. Allen teaches copyright law at Berklee College of Music, where he founded the Rethink Music thinktank and launched the master's degree program in Global Entertainment and Music Business in Valencia, Spain. He also co-founded the music rights data management firm Verifi Media in 2016.

In 2013 to 2014, Allen was a Fellow at the Berkman Klein Center for Internet and Society at Harvard, where he researched new business models for the music industry. He holds a JD and MA from the University of Texas at Austin, and an MA from Northwestern University. He lives in Biarritz, France, where he and his family are renovating a 500 year old Basque farmhouse.

More Fine Publications

Berklee Press

GUITAR

BLUES GUITAR TECHNIQUE
by Michael Williams
50449623 Book/Online Audio $27.99

BERKLEE GUITAR CHORD DICTIONARY
by Rick Peckham
50449546 Jazz – Book $14.99
50449596 Rock – Book.............................$12.99

BERKLEE GUITAR STYLE STUDIES
by Jim Kelly
00200377 Book/Online Media............$24.99

CLASSICAL TECHNIQUE FOR THE MODERN GUITARIST
by Kim Perlak
00148781 Book/Online Audio...............$19.99

CONTEMPORARY JAZZ GUITAR SOLOS
by Michael Kaplan
00143596 Book $16.99

COUNTRY GUITAR STYLES
by Mike Ihde
00254157 Book/Online Audio...............$24.99

CREATIVE CHORDAL HARMONY FOR GUITAR
by Mick Goodrick and Tim Miller
50449613 Book/Online Audio $22.99

FUNK/R&B GUITAR
by Thaddeus Hogarth
50449569 Book/Online Audio.............$19.99

GUITAR SWEEP PICKING
by Joe Stump
00151223 Book/Online Audio................$19.99

JAZZ GUITAR FRETBOARD NAVIGATION
by Mark White
00154107 Book/Online Audio................$19.99

JAZZ GUITAR IMPROVISATION STRATEGIES
by Steven Kirby
00274977 Book/Online Audio.............$24.99

JAZZ SWING GUITAR
by Jon Wheatley
00139935 Book/Online Audio...............$19.99

MODAL VOICINGS FOR GUITAR
by Rick Peckham
00151227 Book/Online Media $19.99

A MODERN METHOD FOR GUITAR*
by William Leavitt
Volume 1: Beginner
00137387 Book/Online Video...............$24.99
Other volumes, media options, and supporting songbooks available.

A MODERN METHOD FOR GUITAR SCALES
by Larry Baione
00199318 Book....................................$12.99

TRIADS FOR THE IMPROVISING GUITARIST
by Jane Miller
00284857 Book/Online Audio.............$19.99

BASS

BASS LINES
Fingerstyle Funk
by Joe Santerre
50449542 Book/Online Audio $19.99
Metal
by David Marvuglio
00122465 Book/Online Audio $19.99
Rock
by Joe Santerre
50449478 Book/Online Audio $22.99

BERKLEE JAZZ BASS
by Rich Appleman, Whit Browne, and Bruce Gertz
50449636 Book/Online Audio $22.99

FUNK BASS FILLS
by Anthony Vitti
50449608 Book/Online Audio...........$22.99

INSTANT BASS
by Danny Morris
50449502 Book/CD $9.99

READING CONTEMPORARY ELECTRIC BASS
by Rich Appleman
50449770 Book...$22.99

VOICE

BELTING
by Jeannie Gagné
00124984 Book/Online Media $19.99

THE CONTEMPORARY SINGER
by Anne Peckham
50449595 Book/Online Audio $27.99

JAZZ VOCAL IMPROVISATION
by Mili Bermejo
00159290 Book/Online Audio $19.99

TIPS FOR SINGERS
by Carolyn Wilkins
50449557 Book/CD $19.95

VOCAL WORKOUTS FOR THE CONTEMPORARY SINGER
by Anne Peckham
50448044 Book/Online Audio...........$24.99

YOUR SINGING VOICE
by Jeannie Gagné
50449619 Book/Online Audio $29.99

WOODWINDS/BRASS

TRUMPET SOUND EFFECTS
by Craig Pederson and Ueli Dörig
00121626 Book/Online Audio...........$14.99

TECHNIQUE OF THE SAXOPHONE
by Joseph Viola
50449820 Volume 1....................................$19.99
50449830 Volume 2....................................$22.99
50449840 Volume 3....................................$22.99

PIANO/KEYBOARD

BERKLEE JAZZ KEYBOARD HARMONY
by Suzanna Sifter
00138874 Book/Online Audio.............$29.99

BERKLEE JAZZ PIANO
by Ray Santisi
50448047 Book/Online Audio $22.99

BERKLEE JAZZ STANDARDS FOR SOLO PIANO
Arranged by Robert Christopherson, Hey Rim Jeon, Ross Ramsay, Tim Ray
00160482 Book/Online Audio.............$19.99

CHORD-SCALE IMPROVISATION FOR KEYBOARD
by Ross Ramsay
50449597 Book/CD.................................$19.99

CONTEMPORARY PIANO TECHNIQUE
by Stephany Tiernan
50449545 Book/DVD $29.99

HAMMOND ORGAN COMPLETE
by Dave Limina
00237801 Book/Online Audio $24.99

JAZZ PIANO COMPING
by Suzanne Davis
50449614 Book/Online Audio $22.99

LATIN JAZZ PIANO IMPROVISATION
by Rebecca Cline
50449649 Book/Online Audio...........$29.99

SOLO JAZZ PIANO
by Neil Olmstead
50449641 Book/Online Audio.............$42.99

DRUMS/PERCUSSION

BEGINNING DJEMBE
by Michael Markus and Joe Galeota
00148210 Book/Online Video...............$16.99

BERKLEE JAZZ DRUMS
by Casey Scheuerell
50449612 Book/Online Audio.............$24.99

DRUM SET WARM-UPS
by Rod Morgenstein
50449465 Book....................................$14.99

DRUM STUDIES
by Dave Vose
50449617 Book..$12.99

A MANUAL FOR THE MODERN DRUMMER
by Alan Dawson and Don DeMichael
50449560 Book...$14.99

MASTERING THE ART OF BRUSHES
by Jon Hazilla
50449459 Book/Online Audio.............$19.99

PHRASING: ADVANCED RUDIMENTS FOR CREATIVE DRUMMING
by Russ Gold
00120209 Book/Online Media $19.99

WORLD JAZZ DRUMMING
by Mark Walker
50449568 Book/CD $22.99

Berklee Press publications feature material developed at the Berklee College of Music.
To browse the complete Berklee Press Catalog, go to **www.berkleepress.com**

STRINGS/ROOTS MUSIC

BERKLEE HARP
Chords, Styles, and Improvisation for Pedal and Lever Harp
by Felice Pomeranz
00144263 Book/Online Audio...........$24.99

BEYOND BLUEGRASS
Beyond Bluegrass Banjo
by Dave Hollander and Matt Glaser
50449610 Book/CD $19.99
Beyond Bluegrass Mandolin
by John McGann and Matt Glaser
50449609 Book/CD $19.99
Bluegrass Fiddle and Beyond
by Matt Glaser
50449602 Book/CD $19.99

CONTEMPORARY CELLO ETUDES
by Mike Block
00159292 Book/Online Audio.............$19.99

EXPLORING CLASSICAL MANDOLIN
by August Watters
00125040 Book/Online Media..........$24.99

FIDDLE TUNES ON JAZZ CHANGES
by Matt Glaser
00120210 Book/Online Audio.............$16.99

THE IRISH CELLO BOOK
by Liz Davis Maxfield
50449652 Book/CD....................$27.99

JAZZ UKULELE
by Abe Lagrimas, Jr.
00121624 Book/Online Audio.............$22.99

BERKLEE PRACTICE METHOD

GET YOUR BAND TOGETHER
With additional volumes for other instruments, plus a teacher's guide.
Bass
by Rich Appleman, John Repucci, and the Berklee Faculty
50449427 Book/CD $19.99
Drum Set
by Ron Savage, Casey Scheuerell, and the Berklee Faculty
50449429 Book/CD $14.95
Guitar
by Larry Baione and the Berklee Faculty
50449426 Book/CD $19.99
Keyboard
by Russell Hoffmann, Paul Schmeling, and the Berklee Faculty
50449428 Book/Online Audio $14.99

MUSIC BUSINESS

CROWDFUNDING FOR MUSICIANS
by Laser Malena-Webber
00285092 Book.......................$17.99

HOW TO GET A JOB IN THE MUSIC INDUSTRY
by Keith Hatschek with Breanne Beseda
00130699 Book.......................$27.99

MAKING MUSIC MAKE MONEY
by Eric Beall
50448009 Book.......................$29.99

MUSIC LAW IN THE DIGITAL AGE
by Allen Bargfrede
00148196 Book.......................$22.99

PROJECT MANAGEMENT FOR MUSICIANS
by Jonathan Feist
50449659 Book.......................$34.99

THE SELF-PROMOTING MUSICIAN
by Peter Spellman
00119607 Book.......................$24.99

MUSIC THEORY/EAR TRAINING/IMPROVISATION

BEGINNING EAR TRAINING
by Gilson Schachnik
50449548 Book/Online Audio $17.99

THE BERKLEE BOOK OF JAZZ HARMONY
by Joe Mulholland and Tom Hojnacki
00113755 Book/Online Audio.............$29.99

BERKLEE CORRESPONDENCE COURSE
00244533 Book/Online Media..........$29.99

BERKLEE EAR TRAINING DUETS AND TRIOS
by Gaye Tolan Hatfield
00284897 Book/Online Audio...........$19.99

BERKLEE MUSIC THEORY
by Paul Schmeling
50449615 Rhythm, Scales Intervals $24.99
50449616 Harmony.....................$24.99

CONDUCTING MUSIC TODAY
by Bruce Hangen
00237719 Book/Online Video.............$24.99

IMPROVISATION FOR CLASSICAL MUSICIANS
by Eugene Friesen with Wendy M. Friesen
50449637 Book/CD $24.99

JAZZ DUETS
by Richard Lowell
00302151 C Instruments.....................$14.99

MUSIC NOTATION
by Mark McGrain
50449399 Theory and Technique....$24.99

REHARMONIZATION TECHNIQUES
by Randy Felts
50449496 Book.......................$29.99

MUSIC PRODUCTION & ENGINEERING

AUDIO MASTERING
by Jonathan Wyner
50449581 Book/CD....................$29.99

AUDIO POST PRODUCTION
by Mark Cross
50449627 Book.......................$19.99

CREATING COMMERCIAL MUSIC
by Peter Bell
00278535 Book/Online Media...........$19.99

THE SINGER-SONGWRITER'S GUIDE TO RECORDING IN THE HOME STUDIO
by Shane Adams
00148211 Book/Online Audio...............$19.99

UNDERSTANDING AUDIO
by Daniel M. Thompson
00148197 Book....................... $42.99

WELLNESS/AUTOBIOGRAPHY

LEARNING TO LISTEN: THE JAZZ JOURNEY OF GARY BURTON
00117798 Book.......................$27.99

MUSICIAN'S YOGA
by Mia Olson
50449587 Book.......................$19.99

THE NEW MUSIC THERAPIST'S HANDBOOK
by Suzanne B. Hanser
00279325 Book.......................$29.99

SONGWRITING/COMPOSING/ARRANGING

ARRANGING FOR HORNS
by Jerry Gates
00121625 Book/Online Audio..............$19.99

ARRANGING FOR STRINGS
by Mimi Rabson
00190207 Book/Online Audio...........$22.99

BEGINNING SONGWRITING
by Andrea Stolpe with Jan Stolpe
00138503 Book/Online Audio $22.99

BERKLEE CONTEMPORARY MUSIC NOTATION
by Jonathan Feist
00202547 Book.......................$24.99

COMPLETE GUIDE TO FILM SCORING
by Richard Davis
50449607 ....$34.99

CONTEMPORARY COUNTERPOINT
by Beth Denisch
00147050 Book/Online Audio...........$24.99

COUNTERPOINT IN JAZZ ARRANGING
by Bob Pilkington
00294301 Book/Online Audio...........$24.99

THE CRAFT OF SONGWRITING
by Scarlet Keys
00159283 Book/Online Audio.............$22.99

CREATIVE STRATEGIES IN FILM SCORING
by Ben Newhouse
00242911 Book/Online Media.............$24.99

JAZZ COMPOSITION
by Ted Pease
50448000 Book/Online Audio $39.99

MELODY IN SONGWRITING
by Jack Perricone
50449419 Book.......................$24.99

MODERN JAZZ VOICINGS
by Ted Pease and Ken Pullig
50449485 Book/Online Audio..........$24.99

MUSIC COMPOSITION FOR FILM AND TELEVISION
by Lalo Schifrin
50449604 Book.......................$39.99

MUSIC NOTATION
50449540 Preparing Scores & Parts.....$24.99
50449399 Theory and Technique...........$24.99

POPULAR LYRIC WRITING
by Andrea Stolpe
50449553 Book.......................$16.99

SONGWRITING: ESSENTIAL GUIDE
by Pat Pattison
50481582 Lyric and Form Structure $19.99
00124366 Rhyming....................$19.99

SONGWRITING IN PRACTICE
by Mark Simos
00244545 Book.......................$16.99

SONGWRITING STRATEGIES
by Mark Simos
50449621 Book.......................$24.99

THE SONGWRITER'S WORKSHOP
by Jimmy Kachulis
50449519 Harmony $29.99
50449518 Melody $24.99